Early Christian Painting

Compass History of Art

Edited by André Held and D. W. Bloemena

The complete series comprises:

Early Christian Painting

Pierre du Bourguet, S. J.
Curator at the Musée du Louvre (Christian Antiquities)

Translated by Simon Watson Taylor

THE VIKING PRESS
New York

A COMPASS BOOKS original edition

Published in 1966 by The Viking Press, Inc.

625 Madison Avenue, New York, N.Y. 10022

Library of Congress catalog card number: 66–10721

Printed in Holland and Switzerland

Contents

Early Christian Painting

Preface

There is one excellent reason for devoting a separate monograph to the history of Early Christian painting, which is that Roman painting did not by any means come to an end with the frescoes of Pompeii and Herculaneum: on the contrary, it continued to develop, in separate pagan and Christian directions, up to and even past the fourth century AD. Even in the East, the almost total obliteration of contemporary evidence is compensated for, to some extent, by ample indications from later times that a very considerable artistic activity existed during this epoch. In terms of artistic inspiration the work with which this present study is concerned may be placed midway between 'Roman' and Byzantine painting. Although Early Christian painting cannot properly be assimilated into either of these artistic movements, its transitional character lends it an added importance, for the very reason that it is situated historically at the crossroads between divergent trends, one looking to the past and the other to the future.

Moreover, this whole body of work has remained largely inaccessible hitherto, for practical reasons. Although various individual aspects have been studied in learned works, or mentioned in the context of later artistic developments, the surviving examples of this art have not previously been grouped comprehensively. As far as Early Christian art in the West is concerned, the paintings of the Roman catacombs are known chiefly through the authoritative work by Mgr. Wilpert, but this rare and costly tome dates from 1903, and the quality of its colour plates is limited by the technical means available at the time, which involved the general use of sketches and reliefs.

Although the documentary evidence is widely scattered, it has proved possible to examine almost all the individual items at first hand, to reproduce them faithfully from the original and to obtain carefully preserved colour values where the usual limitations of a book of this nature have permitted paintings to be reproduced in colour. It should be noted that few of these documents, especially those from Constantinople, Khargeh (Egypt) and North Africa, have hitherto been reproduced in generally accessible form.

The paintings from the Roman catacombs, in particular, may be said to appear for the first time in truly accurate detail in the present volume, and those printed in colour are remarkably faithful to the original colour values. Simply from a scientific point of view, these illustrations provide new and important evidence of the period, and it should perhaps be emphasized that the task of taking photographs of this quality involved a certain measure of physical effort and, at times, personal danger, because of the state of preservation of the catacombs, and the journeys which had to be made through their long, narrow, almost airless corridors.

These subterranean expeditions could not have been undertaken without the gracious courtesy extended to the author and editor by His Holiness Pope Paul VI and the Secretariat of State of the Vatican, and the practical encouragement offered by the Pontifical Commission for Christian Archaeology. The author and editor also wish to take this opportunity to thank all the institutions which facilitated their access to necessary documents.

Introduction

The earliest Christian painting, created in the context of the expiring Roman Empire in the West and in the East, constitutes an impressive body of work. Taking into consideration only the paintings in the Roman catacombs, it may be assigned a role of at least secondary, if not indeed of primary, importance in the category of rock-tomb paintings. It cannot compare, either in quantity or in artistic value, with the rock-tomb paintings of ancient Egypt, but we must remember that the catacomb paintings extend over a far shorter period of time and were created on behalf of one restricted group of citizens.

Early Christian painting has certainly not been ignored in critical works concerned with Christian art. Indeed, it inevitably occupies a prominent place in the pages devoted to Early Christian art, since it provides a considerable number of examples and is, besides, almost certainly the earliest historical manifestation of that art. Even so, one may perhaps question whether the importance of its contribution has been sufficiently recognized. It is true that in the Roman catacombs, for example, the subjects treated achieve little variety and tend to repeat themselves with a degree of monotony liable to discourage even the best intentioned. At first sight, it is the style, above all, which appears repetitive.

In particular, there is no sign of the sharpness of outline and the endlessly renewed variety employed in delineating traditional themes, of the profusion of colours, the sense of movement and liveliness often tinged with humour, which combine to endow its Pharaonic counterparts in Thebes and elsewhere in Egypt with qualities of real greatness in the history of art.

It is a pity, too, that very little of the Early Christian painting of the East has survived. The study of eastern illuminated manuscripts of a much later period makes it clear that one may assume the existence of prototypes during the earliest centuries of the Christian era. The disappearance of this evidence makes any evaluation of Early Christian art necessarily incomplete.

Early Christian art also suffered from the disadvantage that, at the very moment when its own activity was drawing to a close, Byzantine painting was on the verge of a far-reaching advance with the successive development of its two great techniques: mosaic and fresco. On the threshold of this worldly art, which had been in a state of constant evolution for more than eight centuries and which has survived to the present day in those countries which were historically under Byzantine influence, Early Christian painting brings to mind the image of parents of modest extraction and humble means whose son, having achieved fame and wealth, is somewhat embarrassed to produce them in public.

It has, indeed, been claimed more than once that Early Christian painting is devoid of any artistic value. And it must be admitted that the question does arise. It is, in fact, possible to reason that any value it possesses is in proportion to its proximity, especially in Rome and in Italy in general, to the closing phase of Roman art, whereas the inferior technique evident in the decoration of the Roman catacombs, the primitive and barbaric appearance of many of the North African Christian mosaics and the style peculiar to the paintings at Dura-Europos does seem to lend some weight to so derogatory a view.

Even the first discoverers of the catacombs unwittingly debased the reputation in the western world of these works of art by their perfectly well-intentioned but faulty claims on behalf of the material suddenly revealed to them as well as by their simplistic views on the age of these works. When several Roman catacombs suddenly came to light during the sixteenth and seventeenth centuries, after almost ten centuries of oblivion, it was generally thought that the entire subterranean Christian town, and consequently the paintings that decorated it, dated from the time of the persecutions. These discoveries coincided with the first era of the Protestant Reformation, and Catholic theologians thought that they had found here an evident argument in favour of that continuity between the teaching of the ancient Church and that of the modern Church which their adversaries denied.

Although the argument itself was based on perfectly valid principles, and remains, in fact, the basis of extremely interesting researches into the origin of the subjects depicted, the evidence propounded at the time is more than dubious. This attitude of short-sighted apologetics not only warped the course of the studies it inspired but also tended to arouse entrenched suspicions among many people – including Catholic thinkers – about the significance of the themes used in Early Christian creative work, particularly in painting.

These compounded prejudices appear to have had their effect in determining the very minor place generally allotted to Early Christian painting in the history of art, even in the history of Christian art. It is, however, the aim of the present study to show that we have valid grounds for claiming that this period should have a privileged place in the history of art and more particularly in that of Christian art.

The Importance of Early Christian Painting

The first important factor to consider in relation to Early Christian painting is that it constitutes, in the West and in part of the East, though in a non-pagan context, the final stage of Roman painting. Contemporary art history no longer subscribes to the derogatory view that all so-called decadent periods are devoid of any artistic value whatsoever. In the first place, the canons of art change with the times; in the second place, a period labelled decadent often clarifies from an artistic point of view the summit of which it constitutes the downward slope and, at the same time, it may contain the first outlines of the new summit which the historian perceives on the horizon.

Although Early Christian painting is of prime importance in the history of Early Christian iconography as such, there are several other art forms that should be taken into account when studying this particular period. Apart from innumerable sarcophagus reliefs, certain ivory statuettes and other minor art objects (such as 'gold-glass' bases, terracotta lamps and tiles, bone combs and liturgical boxes, ivory pyxides and intaglios) deserve to be taken into consideration. But in terms of quantity or size they cannot be compared with the pictorial work of the same period. And besides, one may well ask whether sculpture, particularly relief work, where the space is reduced by an immediate background, is not generally, in the last analysis, simply the projection into space of a two-dimensional art.

Nevertheless, there is no doubt that, however modest its ultimate origin, the iconographic foundation of Christian art was henceforward to be that exemplified in the catacombs, mausoleums and churches of the

Early Christian era. This is particularly true in the East because of the prolonged Byzantine influence there, but is equally true of the various western centres of artistic production contemporary with those of Byzantium. In Byzantium, for example, Early Christian painting might well exalt the sovereignty of Christ by endowing the image with the Imperial emblems, an attribution designed to emphasize that the work was a reflection, on the aesthetic plane, of a theocratic political system. The fact remains that the actual process through which this new iconography was elaborated preceded the formation of the Byzantine artistic centre and, indeed, of all the other centres of Christian art.

It is true that the surviving artistic evidence is predominantly western, and the very rarity of eastern examples renders any list of Early Christian painting necessarily sketchy. It deserves to be attempted, nevertheless, because it is precisely in the Early Christian period that the first realistic depictions are to be found of the figures of Christ, the Virgin, the Apostles and the martyrs, and this applies equally to the first successful attempts at composing scenes which bring together various personages from the Gospels and even the Old Testament. No matter that these images and compositions are frequently clumsy or sketchy, that they lack movement and remain in some respects strongly influenced by Roman or eastern imagery and composition: their importance lies in the fact that they represent the passage from the idea or tale to the depiction. They are the projection on the pictorial plane of the person of Christ, of the Virgin and of the Apostles and martyrs, just as they had appeared hitherto in the text of the Gospels and in the minds of their contemporaries or of the other faithful. Consequently, the role of Early Christian painting in the elaboration of these themes remains of prime importance, despite the total lack of surviving work from the East, although this lack cannot be disregarded. Naturally these early models were destined to become transformed with the passage of time, not only into Byzantine art, but equally into Romanesque art, Gothic art and the styles born of the Renaissance, just as they are transformed into abstract art today and will continue in the future to be subject to the fresh approaches of African, Asian and American artists, whether or not they happen to be Christians, who will impose new shapes and features on these figures and compositions. There is only a difference of degree between the originally constituted image and that same image reproduced with however many modifications. But the passage from thought to representation involves a leap from one plane to another, and that leap contains an element of the infinite. This essential transformation occurred during the period which concerns us.

In the same way, Early Christian painting is largely dominated by the first examples of figural Christian art. Every attempt at representation obeys a certain aesthetic ideal. Whatever may have been that of the first Christians, it must inevitably reveal itself beneath these hesitant beginnings. Despite the awkwardness of their techniques, the first Christians did impart certain tendencies to art. However embryonic these may have been, and however much they may have inherited elements from pre-Christian times, or reflected the manner of life of the society in which the artists were involved, they not only have survived the transformations imposed by the exigencies of time and place but retain a lasting validity. These tendencies are, indeed, bound up with a new perception of things, which derives from the very essence of Christianity.

The iconography of the first Christians, as indeed all non-Christian art of the same period, was bound to contain an element of symbolism. All the artist could do was to attempt to translate the invisible, such as he imagined it, in terms of the visible. In addition to new themes, the creators of Early Christian art introduced into the interpretation and expression of the forms their surroundings offered them a new visual approach which was destined to impart a firm and lasting direction to the manifestations of all art of Christian inspiration throughout the world and over the centuries. Thus, here too, Early Christian painting must be considered to have played an initiatory role, and simply to mention the fact, whatever may be the aesthetic value of its productions, is to stress its far-ranging importance. Had the first Christians been unfaithful to their doctrine in the representational means they used, then the entire spirit of Christian art and, no doubt, its value for succeeding ages, would have been radically altered.

It must be remembered that iconography does not simply imply an aesthetically oriented perception of reality. Through the personages and objects represented, it also bears constant witness to its own epoch. Since these pictorial works were designed to decorate the earliest sanctuaries, or to honour a particular martyr, or were created on behalf of a deceased person and of those who came to visit the tomb in the depths of these necropolises, the testimony bears primarily upon these Christians, upon the degree to which they understood the message of Christ and even upon the choice they may have made of Biblical, Evangelical or other subjects. They thus make a considerable contribution to our knowledge of primitive Christianity and of its already established traditions.

Although Christians were partially separated by their religious ideals from the society of their time, they still retained important bonds with it through their inevitable membership of various social spheres. The surrounding world filtered through with the Christians into the catacombs, as it did into the 'ecclesial houses' of the period of the persecutions; and it penetrated more openly into the first official churches of the Christian era. In the obscurity of the necropolis and the subdued light of the sanctuary, Early Christian painting is the reflection of those social spheres and of the epoch as a whole.

Within these perspectives, the importance of Early Christian painting assumes its proper dimensions. It was almost inevitable that, together with the reliefs carved on sarcophagi, it became the most important means of figural expression available to the Christians. The large-scale works, together with the reliefs, constitute the first known repository of Christian iconography, and everything that followed it in the course of time must be considered its heir.

The Distribution of This Painting

The diffusion of the Gospel was accomplished in the Mediterranean periphery during the first two centuries, and it gave rise everywhere to figural representations. Though it is true that the Roman catacombs have provided most of the evidence, nevertheless surviving Christian edifices, in the East as well as in the West, have made a particular contribution which should not be ignored. For this reason, an inventory of the principal monuments of Christian inspiration is plainly necessary. The architecture in question is not only extremely diverse but alters perceptibly even during the course of the period which concerns us.

Places of Worship

The Christians' first meeting places were private houses, as is attested by the Acts of the Apostles, the Epistles of St Paul and the writings of Tertullian, among others, in the third century. However simple these premises may originally have been, which were simply lent for the occasion, it seems likely that some owners may eventually have decided to set aside one house or another exclusively for purposes of worship, and as a result the need would quite naturally have been felt for an appropriate decorative scheme.

The proof of this may perhaps be furnished by the Christian house of Dura-Europos, a caravan halting-place on the frontier between Syria and Mesopotamia. Adjoining a synagogue which is itself decorated with scenes from the Old Testament (figs. 167–70) and dates, likewise, from the middle of the third century, it consisted of two rooms which must have served respectively as meeting place and baptistry. This identification may be made with certainty because of the nature of the scenes from the Old and New Testaments which decorate the walls of the second room, all of them being thematically linked with the salvation of the soul and most of them with the liturgy of Baptism (figs. 165 and 166).

This double utilization of a private house is a sufficiently strong indication that the same practice occurred elsewhere, particularly in Rome. But no baptistry has ever been found in that city anterior to the 'Peace of the Church' which resulted from the adoption of Christianity by Constantine as the official religion of the Roman Empire. Any baptistries of that time, which were probably decorated with themes similar to those just described, doubtless vanished, together with the houses which provided the first meeting places, beneath churches erected during the fourth century. It must be said that the hypothesis of the existence of baptistries in the Roman catacombs rests solely on the discovery in the Catacomb of St Pontianus (via Portuensis) of a baptistry which cannot be earlier than the fifth century, and on the presence in several catacombs of wells capable of providing water for ceremonial as well as for everyday purposes. It is, in any case, far more probable that baptistries should have formed part of a church or an 'ecclesial house' rather than of a necropolis.

This original form of ecclesial house must, it is generally believed, have given way to a larger and more complex form under the impulsion of two circumstances. First, the number of Christian believers increased very rapidly and small houses no longer provided sufficient space. Secondly, people of wealth and substance became converts and hastened to proffer their mansions as meeting places for Christian congregations. Such mansions were, indeed, admirably suited to these purposes. In that era they contained a *vestibulum* leading to an *atrium*, beyond which were situated the hearth and altar of the *lararia*; then came a *tablinum* and, at each side or beyond it, a long narrow room, the *triclinium*, the roof of which was supported by rows of columns. The atrium and tablinum were probably used by the Christians for communal prayer, and the triclinium for the celebration of the Eucharist, these being the two fundamental activities of the Christian liturgy. These mansions were decorated; portraits of ancestors or *imagines clipeatae* (replicas of which exist in the shape of the medallions of the Popes in the Basilica of St Paul) ornamented the atrium; mosaics spread their designs over the surface of the ground just as they later studded the floors of certain churches – for example that of Kabr Hiram in Phoenicia – and the fonts of certain baptistries – for example, that of a baptistry in the Kelibia region, now in the Bardo Museum in Tunis. The walls of the houses of Pompeii and Herculaneum were covered with paintings, as we know.

There was, then, an almost imperceptible transition from the ecclesial house to the basilica, and, whatever may have been their exact origin, from the beginning of the fourth century onwards basilicas were widely incorporated into new building projects, especially in imperial constructions in large cities. The churches of Pudentienna and Maria Maggiore, among many others in Rome, both founded in the fourth century, and that of Sabina, founded in the fifth century, still retain some original mosaics; those in the first church, though since restored, date from the end of the fourth century, and in the other two from the fifth. Finally, in

Palestine (figs. 161 and 162) and in North Africa, a few churches have yielded fifth-century mosaics, and the mosaics to be found in certain churches in Antioch, Syria, may well date back to that era (fig. 164).

Other architectural projects for places of worship were drawn up from the beginning of the fourth century onwards. Quite apart from the churches of cruciform outline and the *martyria* (places where the faithful celebrated the martyr's feast day) – among which one must mention a *martyrium* oratory in Milan, as well as a baptistry (fig. 140) in the same town, both decorated with mosaics – mausoleums were erected in designs taking their inspiration from the constructions dedicated by the Romans to their heroes. Among the best known and most magnificently adorned with mosaics is the church of S. Costanza (St Constantina, the daughter of Constantine) in Rome, dating from the fourth century, in which the decoration of the ambulatory is still well preserved, though originally there were mosaics in the cupola which are known to us today only through later drawings. Other mausoleums which deserve mention include that of Centcelles in Spain, and that of the Empress Galla Placidia, mother of Valentinian III, in Ravenna. Two small square-shaped constructions akin to mausoleums are to be found in the Khargeh oasis in Egypt, and each of these is surmounted by a cupola decorated with paintings.

In considering these fourth- and fifth-century mosaics in general, it should be emphasized that only those from S. Costanza in Rome and from the tombstone slabs of Tabarca in Tunisia may properly be considered to qualify as Early Christian art. The others, as well as the few surviving illuminated manuscripts from this epoch, should be viewed in the perspective of a fresh awareness of reality which formed the prelude to Byzantine art, and are mentioned here for reasons of comparison and indeed, to indicate elements of basic divergence.

The Catacombs

It seems that the catacombs, unlike the private houses and mansions, were not, on the whole, used by the Christians as meeting places, and in normal times such use must have been limited to occasional visits, to celebrate the anniversary of particular martyrs. During periods of violent persecution the early Christians may have gathered there to avoid endangering the community through open assembly, and finally, after the Peace of the Church, for reasons of pilgrimage. The subterranean churches to be found in certain catacombs date from after the Peace. Outside these churches there was not sufficient space in the catacombs to permit any large-scale assembly.

With its network of tiered galleries, the catacomb constitutes a funerary scheme unique to Christianity. Pre-Christian as well as Christian necropolises, whether of Etruscan, Jewish (figs. 131–33) or Egyptian origin, all establish the same pattern of a series of tombs comprising at most a few chambers strictly isolated from each other, communication between some of them being the result either of chance or of the activities of tomb-robbers. The catacombs, on the other hand, were hollowed out of the rock in response to a particular need, and the digging processes rapidly became systematic. Several attempts have been made to analyse their beginnings. It is important to remember, first of all, that the number of Christians continued to increase throughout the second and third centuries, despite the persecutions.

But is is essential, above all else, to remember that Christianity found repugnant the practice of cremation then in wide use among the Romans, and this for good reasons: the Christian dogma of the resurrection of the body was reinforced in those early times by a somewhat primitive belief that this process required that the corpse's physical integrity be preserved; moreover, it was felt that bodies made holy by martyrdom and sanctified by baptism ought to be treated with great respect. As a result of this attitude, an ever-increasing need developed for extensive burial-places.

It is possible, and has been suggested, that the Roman social framework, because of the existence within it of the category of 'clients' (dependents), was able to provide the means for this necessary expansion. Families of the Roman aristocracy owned plots of land, outside the city walls, acquired in accordance with the law, and had themselves buried in the mausoleum or hypogeum built thereon. The latter form of funerary monument was a tomb composed of one or several subterranean chambers where sarcophagi or funeral urns stood in wall-recesses. The outside entrance, at ground level, was inscribed with the owner's name. The family of that original owner, whose remains were secure inside the hypogeum or above ground in the mausoleum as the case might be, had the legal right to add, over the years, the mortal remains not only of members of the family but also of his 'clients'. Any Christian owner of such a tomb was certainly prepared to include his less fortunate co-religionists in this category of 'clients'.

Nevertheless, one major difficulty stands in the way of this hypothesis – the analysis of the ground in those sites which have been most thoroughly examined points to the initial independence of the catacomb in relation to the particular hypogeum to which it became subsequently connected. If, then, one cannot exclude the possibility of the extension of an ancient hypogeum, the fact remains that, even before the third century, certain groups of Christians were also able to share the privilege accorded to the guilds of establishing their own communal cemetery. In both cases, when the ground surface was no longer capable of containing the number of Christian bodies or of satisfying the necessity for ensuring that the corpse retained its physical integrity as far as possible, the logical solution adopted was to dig down deeper under the surface of the property: one might say that in terms of height today's skyscrapers are the equivalent of the catacombs, providing on behalf of the living the same sort of answer to the problem of space limitation.

A description of the method of excavation will make clear how this new concept was implemented. First of all, a flight of steps was dug out of the ground. At the level of the bottom step a horizontal corridor was hollowed out, running parallel and at equal depth to one side of the plot's surface; at the boundary point, an extension was dug at right angles to the end of the first, and this new corridor was joined at regular intervals by other corridors parallel to the first one. Depending on specific needs, further flights of steps would be carved out of the rock leading to other storeys of similar networks.

It goes without saying that this is a much simplified description of the process, which disregards the interruptions, twists and turns, changes in gallery level, and other complexities of lay-out. In the crypt of the hypogeum, reserved for the owner's family, marble sarcophagi containing the corpses were usually placed beneath a blind arcade hollowed out of the wall. Sometimes a long series of chapels was created with funerary chambers on each side (fig. 118). In most instances, the walls of these galleries were reserved for the interment of the Christian 'clients' or, at least, of members of the Christian community. Niche-shaped semi-circular recesses (*arcosolia*) provided receptacles for these bodies, either in the gallery's actual wall, or in *cubicula* (small rooms with space for several burial-places) hollowed out of the wall. In order to make use of all available space, the walls were often riddled with row upon row of regularly spaced *loculi*, holes in the form of rectangular boxes of equal depth. Such was the form of a completed catacomb.

Catacomb painting covered the walls of those hypogea connected with the cemetery, the arcosolia, and, within the cubicula, the vaulted ceilings and the walls. In this connection, it is important to determine, as far as this is possible, what inspired the Christians to decorate the arcosolia of the galleries and the cubicula with paintings.

The most widely held opinion today is that the idea was inherited from the practices of the Jews of the Diaspora and, in particular, of the Jewish community of Rome. The common objection that the Jews were categorically forbidden to execute any artistic reproductions does not, in fact, hold good any longer, as far as the period under discussion is concerned. The decorated synagogue of Dura-Europos furnishes one of several examples; others include the Jewish cemetery of the Via Appia in Rome and the Necropolis of Gamart in Carthage. If a current of Jewish thought more closely attached to tradition was able to transmit to some categories of Christians a certain mistrust of representations of the human form, it is equally possible that another more emancipated trend of Jewish thought existed as well, one that was more receptive to Christian ideas and reciprocally capable of exercising considerable influence upon the liturgical behaviour of budding Christianity. This important line of research, which should have been adopted for *a priori* reasons, has been long neglected, despite the fact that evidence of the use by the Christians of symbols of Jewish origin is becoming increasingly clear. It seems probable, though not yet proven, that Jewish paintings of scenes featuring human figures predated the Early Christian paintings in the catacombs. In any case, the hypothesis is rich in possibilities for future research.

Such a hypothesis, however, appears too restricted to the acceptance of an evolution of ideas and practices in a closed environment, and takes too little account of the influence on Rome of the funerary customs of the Etruscans and the Southern Italians. One particular Etruscan rock-cut tomb, that of the Typhon in Tarquinia, contains figural painted friezes dating from the end of the second century BC, and the painted tombs of southern Italy go back at least as far as the beginning of the second century BC. If we compare these painted tombs with those Roman hypogea in Alexandria and Rome and the funerary houses of Tuna el Gibel in Egypt, which were also decorated with paintings, we must inevitably consider the alternative hypothesis that in the West a peninsular tradition influenced, indeed, by the Eastern practices which had then become fashionable and, above all, by the Jewish hypogea, ultimately affected the hypogea attached to the Christian necropolises, and that this influence was then naturally transmitted to the necropolises themselves. It seems that we must be satisfied with these conjectures about the origins of Christian tomb-painting.

Although the greater number of catacombs decorated with paintings are situated in Rome, they are also to be found scattered throughout the countries bordering the Mediterranean. It is not the intention of the present study to draw up an exhaustive list of the various catacombs existing in the Christian world of that era apart from those in Rome. But it is worth while indicating the principal centres, since their distribution serves to cast some light on certain aspects of the pictorial art of the epoch. It may also be noted that in addition to their wall-paintings several of these catacombs contain mosaics.

In Rome, the most important catacombs are situated to the north and south-east of the town. In the north, the Catacomb of Priscilla is to be found in the Via Salaria Nuova not far from those of St Felicity, Thraso and the Jordani. In the south, the Via Appia contains, in a compact grouping, the Catacomb of Callixtus, St Sebastian *ad catacumbas* and the Catacomb of Praetextatus, followed by the Catacomb of Domitilla, which is situated in the Via Ardeatina at the point where it leaves the Via Appia — these four catacombs forming a veritable subterranean city. In the south-east, between these two massive groups, a recently discovered cemetery, the New Catacomb of the Via Latina, contains a large number of wall-paintings. Apart from these groups of primary importance, a few others deserve to be mentioned: to the north-west, in the Via Salaria Vecchia, the catacombs of St Pamphilus and Clodius Hermes (the latter also known as the Catacomb of Basilla); to the north-east, in the Via Nomentana, the *Coemeterium Maius;* to the south-east, that of St. Peter and St Marcellinus; to the far south, in the Via Ostiensis, the Catacomb of Commodilla; to the south-west, in the Via Portuensis, the Catacomb of Pontianus.

Outside Rome, there still exist in Naples several catacombs in a poor state of preservation, including that of St Januarius. Sicily originally possessed many catacombs, the most important surviving ones, at Syracuse, being that of S. Giovanni, typical of fourth-century construction, and those of S. Maria di Gesu and of Cassia, which are somewhat earlier in date. There is at least one catacomb still to be seen in Yugoslavia, that in Niš (fig. 141).

The catacombs in Malta, of which there are several, including that of S. Paolo, are reminiscent of Phoenician tombs. In Spain, one fourth-century mausoleum is still to be seen in Centcelles. In North Africa a number of catacombs have survived, including those of Sallakta and Hadrumetum in Tunisia, and funerary mosaics, particularly in Kelibia in Souk-el-Abiod (fig. 163) and in Tabarca.

It is interesting to note that in Egypt, the land of rock-tombs, no catacombs have been discovered other than those in Alexandria, that most Greco-Roman of cities, and among these vanished constructions the only one of which we know anything is the no longer extant catacomb of Karmuz, through surviving sketches of the wall-paintings.

Further to the East, we find a funerary chamber in Sidon and the fourth-century necropolis of Seleucia.

Since 'gold-glass' and illuminations, like mosaics, form a constituent part of Early Christian painting, it is necessary to mention them at this point. The 'gold-glass' portrait medallions (figs. 143 and 144) were generally set in the lime which sealed the compartments in the catacombs, where they served as recognition marks for relatives; or sometimes had a purely decorative purpose. Illuminations dating back to this period are extremely rare, and the only one still known to us is an illuminated Greek manuscript from Alexandria, in a bad state of preservation, now in the Moscow Museum (fig. 171).

To this should be added the late fourth-century Berlin *Itala*, the *Iliad*

of the Milan Ambrosiana, and the two fifth-century Vatican Virgils, because, despite their secular nature and new character, they show a style
common to both pagan and Christian art of the fifth century.

It is within this rather broad perspective that we must consider the col-
ouring techniques used during the Early Christian era. Two techniques
were used at this time for the execution of actual paintings: fresco and
tempera (distemper painting). The bed-rock of the catacombs tended to
be far from solid, and unlike the painted wall surfaces of Pompeii and
Herculaneum, could generally take only one layer of coating: this was
composed of lime and volcanic dust (pozzolana) diluted with slaked lime.
In certain catacombs, however, including those of Domitilla, Praetextatus
and Clodius Hermes, a two-layered coating is to be found, the undersurface being pozzolana, with a mixture of pozzolana and powdered
marble spread on top. At Dura-Europos, the undersurface is composed of
chalk and sand, and the top surface of chalk, the porousness of the chalk
permitting distemper-painting.

Painting equipment of the time is described to us in the Catacomb of
Callixtus, where an inscription lists compasses, stylet and two paint-
brushes. The painting surface and the border were usually sketched out
with the aid of the compasses, the brush or stylet then outlined the figures
and finally the details were added.

Mosaic involved inlaying still-moist plaster with comparatively small
enamelled cubes. The mosaicist was preceded in his work by the painter,
who sketched out beforehand on the prepared surface the figures of the
theme to be designed.

The preparation of the cubes of gold that were to be employed increasingly in Byzantine mosaic offers analogies with the preparation of the gold
inlay for the base of drinking vessels or 'gold-glasses'. In the first instance,
a leaf of metal was wrapped around a cube of transparent glass; in the
second, a leaf of gold, cut to represent the proposed design, was inserted
between two thin sheets of glass which had already been slightly moulded
to the necessary outline, several strata being then welded in the furnace.

The Subjects Represented

A survey of the subjects and designs represented in Early Christian pictorial art is an essential preliminary to any study, and some kind of classification, however arbitrary it may be, will not only be instructive but also
serve to provide a perspective. Classification is rendered necessary in this
instance because many of the subjects represented are unvaried between
one monument and another and, very occasionally, between one catacomb and another, whereas some others appear episodically (taking into

account the possible discovery of new catacombs such as, for instance, that of the Via Latina, first revealed in 1955). Within these limitations, it is of some interest to note the approximate date when a particular subject first appeared or finally disappeared. It will be appropriate, therefore, at this stage, to draw up a subject list which, while not aiming to be exhaustive, will nonetheless encompass the main themes of Early Christian painting.

The dating of this work, though not arbitrary, does remain relative. The absence of any actually indicated dates makes it necessary to resort to extrinsic criteria: that is to say, the period during which part of a building was constructed or part of a catacomb was excavated in relation to other parts already dated by an inscription; or, in catacombs, the manufacturer's mark stamped on the bricks forming part of a particular piece of wall; or the stylistic similarity of the paintings or mosaics with that of contemporary pictorial works. Here it is necessary to anticipate considerations elaborated later in this study in order to indicate that the period we are dealing with starts not earlier than the beginning of the third century and that the fourth century, it should be remembered, brought profound changes in Roman society even before the Peace of the Church and the fresh impetus which the Edict of Milan provided for the entire field of artistic expression.

Finally, it must be emphasized that not all of the subjects in the following sections are indubitably of Christian origin. Most of the hypogea which developed into Christian catacombs or which contained the bodies of Christians belonged to families whose members were not necessarily all Christians, and any pagan members retained the privilege of being buried in the family hypogeum and having their tomb decorated in any way that pleased them.

Christ

The iconography of Christ reflected, initially, a certain hesitancy which may have its origin in the reticent attitude inherent in Judeo-Christian society, but which may equally be attributed to the respect felt for his person and to the difficulty of deciding definitively upon suitable features for him. Apart from the well-known symbols of the Fish (figs. 11 and 162) and the Lamb, it seems that the most ancient representations were provided by the figures of the Good Shepherd and of Orpheus charming the animals (figs. 12 and 27). These figures are also symbolic and will be considered later in this aspect, but because of the importance they assume in the general iconography of Christ it is necessary to mention them at this juncture.

Because the main figure is almost invariably surrounded by lambs or goats, it is not always so easy for us to distinguish between the two themes as it seems to have been for the early Christians. The recent analysis of a manuscript from Qumran, near the Dead Sea, appears to provide a full explanation of the origin of the representation of Christ as Orpheus. A poem of probably Essenian origin, put into the mouth of King David and containing allusions to the Greek Zitherist's myth, seems to have been at the origin of the conception of David-Orpheus as the prefiguration of the *new* David, the Christ-Orpheus.

The theme of the Good Shepherd is not only repeated constantly upon the walls and vault of the Roman catacombs, but it also occurs very frequently throughout the Mediterranean area and the neighbouring regions, from Dura-Europos, through the Mausoleum of the Exodus in the Khargeh oasis (fig. 152), to the monuments of Cyrene, Tabarca (fig. 160) and Campania. And it was destined to remain a favourite theme in these regions for many centuries.

From the third century onwards, nevertheless, there is a tendency to transform pure symbolism by adding to the conventional scene some new element with a purely mystical connotation, such as that of fishes (Cyrene, the grotto in the necropolis). This kind of modification nevertheless led to a greater realism, as when the Shepherd among his flock begins to assume a stance recognizably similar to that ascribed to Christ in the New Testament, perhaps dispensing his teachings (fig. 36). This development was doubtless prompted by the desire to encourage those of the faithful called to martyrdom to put their trust in the person of Christ: it was, in fact, at about this time that the miracles and scenes from the Scriptures began to be depicted. Favourite themes were the Multiplication of Loaves and Fishes, the Breaking of the Bread, the Good Samaritan, and various miracles: the Woman Diseased with an Issue of Blood, the Man Sick with the Palsy, the Woman Bent Double, the Lepers, the Man Blind from Birth, the Marriage at Cana and, most frequently, the Raising of Lazarus. It may be noted that in the Catacomb of Praetextatus Christ is portrayed protecting his disciples against Satan. The Baptism of Christ (fig. 9) provides an equally important message of encouragement, emphasizing that the Christian belongs to his Master, since baptism applies the divine seal of his teachings upon his flock. The Christ Crowned with Thorns (?) (fig. 53) of the Catacomb of Praetextatus marks an accentuation of the realism that was to become increasingly apparent during the fourth and fifth centuries.

From the fourth century onwards, other scenes such as the miraculous catch of fish and the healing of a man possessed of the devil were added; but an increased importance was now particularly assigned to the theme already indicated in the paintings in the hypogeum of the Aurelians and in Cyrene, that of Christ's mission of teaching. Here is Christ represented in person surrounded by his disciples, delivering the Sermon on the Mount (New Catacomb of the Via Latina), giving the law to St Peter

(Grotta Ferrata), teaching St Paul (New Catacomb of the Via Latina), crowning a martyr (St Sebastian *ad catacumbas*), dividing the ten virgins into two groups (Catacomb of St Cyriacus), appearing, in fact, as Doctor and Judge. But his glorious role is equally emphasized: in the pre-Constantinian necropolis of the Vatican, he is already depicted in mosaic as the sun in his chariot (fig. 130), and in Naples, in the Catacomb of St Januarius, he is represented in his Ascension. Finally, he appears in majesty in the Catacomb of Domitilla (fig. 35), and that of St Peter and St Marcellinus (fig. 90), and there is a bust of Christ in the Catacomb of Commodilla (fig. 22).

Beardless up to the fourth century, he is now represented as being bearded. His clothes have changed, too. Hitherto clothed as the Shepherd in an *exomis*, a short tunic leaving the right shoulder bare, he henceforward wears the *pallium*. It is significant in this connection that in a painting in the Catacomb of Hermes dating from the middle of the third century the Good Shepherd is shown wearing imperial robes. These various modifications indicate a new visual perception. Respect for transcendence, as well as the influence of late Jewish tradition, had probably led artists to depict Christ in terms of the idealized appearance of the Greek gods or heroes such as Aristaeus Criophorus or Orpheus, a concept imbued with a wholly ingenuous mysticism and exalted by the atmosphere of persecution. When this atmosphere gave way to a more normal climate of opinion, this deep respect became transposed to a more concrete plane, the prevalent feeling of the time, that is akin to the expression of respect due from subjects to the Emperor.

The Virgin Mary

The model invoked by Christians in depicting the Virgin Mary appears to have become definitive at a very early stage. This is rather surprising since, even more, perhaps, than in the case of Christ, the model had to be invented. The representations of gods or of deified men, such as Orpheus, Aristaeus, Jupiter, and also those of men actively engaged in the manifold activities of everyday life, could reasonably provide a choice of types from which representations of Christ might be fashioned. But this was by no means the case as regards the idea of maternity, or at least the quest was more complicated. Aphrodite and Eros, as usually portrayed, were entirely unsuitable models, and it seems possible that it was found necessary to derive inspiration from representations of some less celebrated goddess, Pomona perhaps, or a foreign goddess, Isis, mother of Horus, whose somewhat esoteric cult was fashionable at that time throughout the countries bordering the Mediterranean.

Except, obviously, in the scene of the Annunciation (Catacomb of

Priscilla), Mary is always represented with the Infant Jesus. In the scene of the Nativity (St Sebastian *ad catacumbas*), she is depicted close to the Christ Child. But in most instances she is seated and holding him to her breast, possibly suckling him (Catacomb of Priscilla), not far from an *orans* (fig. 70), or else showing him to the people present. These witnesses are very often the Magi, their number varying according to the space available, sometimes two (fig. 88), sometimes three or even four, although the usual number was three, presumably because of the number of gifts mentioned in the Scriptures. In one painting in the Catacomb of Priscilla, in the gallery of a *crypta arenaria*, upon an ornamented tomb (fig. 66), Mary is placed near a standing figure pointing with one arm towards a star; this figure was previously thought to be Isaiah, but it has now been positively identified with Balaam. The subject is, in any case, to all intents and purposes an invention symbolizing for Christians the profound mystery of the union of the two Testaments.

The Old Testament

It is indeed very probable that this symbolic union influenced, at least in the earliest times, the choice of subjects taken from the Old Testament. The allegorical significance of Biblical characters and events was, in any case, heavily emphasized by the Fathers of the Church, from St Paul and Christ himself onwards. It is not always easy today to detect that quality in these early paintings. Nevertheless, in order to complete the list of subjects relevant to the Christ figure, it is important to note, even at the risk of anticipating a later section of this study, that several of these personages must have been interpreted by contemporary artists as representations of the Saviour. This is certainly true of the scene of Moses Striking the Rock (also at S. Constanza), of the Sacrifice of Isaac, of Jonah (also at Khargeh, Mausoleum of the Exodus), and on various 'gold-glasses', of Job himself (also at Khargeh), of the Shepherd and his Flock (*idem*), of the Agony of Isaiah (*idem*).

Subjects borrowed from the Old Testament may well have formed the majority of those represented from the beginning of the Early Christian period up to the Peace of the Church. A list of the most ancient subjects would include: the Temptation of Adam and Eve, Noah in the Ark, the Sacrifice of Isaac, Balaam Pointing at the Star, David Carrying his Sling, the Ascension of Elijah, Susanna and the Elders (also at Khargeh), Daniel in the Lions' Den (*idem*), the Three Hebrews in the Fiery Furnace (*idem*), Tobias and the Fish.

It is not true, as has been claimed, that these subjects disappear with the establishment of the Peace of the Church and the advent of history painting: they are all still to be found during the fourth century – for example, in the New Catacomb of the Via Latina – except for the theme of Tobias and the Fish, and even that is depicted in the Mausoleum of Constantius, and, in two scenes, in the Catacomb of Thraso.

On the other hand, a number of new episodes do appear during the fourth century, and some of these show such complicated detail that it would seem they may have been based on earlier manuscript illuminations. Among these new themes, the following may be mentioned: Adam and Eve Entering Eden (Khargeh) or Driven out by the Angel, or Overwhelmed with Sadness in the Presence of Cain or Abel Bearing Offerings (New Catacomb of the Via Latina) (fig. 125); the Offerings of Cain and Abel (originally in the Mausoleum of S. Costanza); the Flood (New Catacomb of the Via Latina); Noah Supervising the Building of the Ark (originally in the Mausoleum of S. Costanza); the Drunkenness of Noah, the Flight from Sodom with Lot's Wife Transformed into a Pillar of Salt (New Catacomb of the Via Latina); the Meal of Isaac; Rebecca and Eliezer (Khargeh) (fig. 153); the Vision of Abraham beside the Mamre Oaks (fig. 120); Jacob and the Vision of Bethel (fig. 128); the Two Dreams of Joseph, Joseph Welcoming his Brothers, the Arrival of Jacob and his Sons in Egypt (fig. 123); Jacob Blessing Ephraim and Manasseh, the Angel Stopping Balaam's Ass (fig. 114); Moses Rescued from the River (fig. 122); the Crossing of the Red Sea (New Catacomb of the Via Latina) (figs. 124 and 127); the Pursuit of the Hebrews by the Egyptians (Khargeh) (fig. 153); Moses Putting on His Shoes (New Catacomb of the Via Latina); Moses Before the Burning Bush (Khargeh); the Jews Rebelling against Moses and Aaron (New Catacomb of the Via Latina); a Jew Escorting Moses as the Latter Strikes the Rock (Catacomb of Callixtus) (fig. 8); Jethro Rejoining Moses in Sinai (Khargeh); Rahab Welcoming the Messengers of Joshua (a vanished mosaic originally in the cupola of the Mausoleum of S. Costanza); the Samson cycle – wrestling with two lions (fig. 109), creating fear in the hearts of the Philistines (fig. 115), sending wolves among their crops); Absalom Caught by his Hair in a Tree (New Catacomb of the Via Latina); the Three Hebrews Refusing to Worship Nebuchadnezzar's Image (Catacomb of Priscilla, Hypogeum of Glabrio); the Executioner Feeding the Flames of the Furnace in which the Three Hebrews are calling upon the Lord, Job and Job's Wife (New Catacomb of the Via Latina); Isaiah Sawn in Two (Khargeh); the Sacrifice of Elijah (a single representation, no longer surviving, in the Mausoleum of S. Costanza); Jeremiah Lamenting Jerusalem (Khargeh) (fig. 151).

It remains true that with the establishment of the Peace of the Church, history painting did tend to supplant the earlier painting of primarily symbolic inspiration. The cycle of the Crossing of the Red Sea (figs. 124 and 127) and that of Samson (figs. 109 and 115), and the paintings in the New Catacomb of the Via Latina, the tendency to isolate individual figures within the picture's design or, alternatively, to depict crowds, all lead to a narrative painting in the historical sense. But this new approach only achieved full impetus in the fifth century, with the mosaic work in S. Maria Maggiore. Here, the upper frieze on each side of the nave depicts the history of the Israelites from Abraham to Joshua: forty-four episodes, fifteen of which were destroyed or have been replaced by fresco paintings, follow each other in clear sequence. With these mosaics a new direction was created which was to assume its full importance in Byzantine painting and mosaic work.

The costumes depicted made no pretence at re-creating historical truth, being invariably the clothes worn in the artist's own time, and often chosen by him as appropriate for the particular action or role assigned to the figure in question. For example: Tobias in the scene with the fish has his loins swathed in the *ventrale*, like a professional fisherman; Abraham is dressed in the *paenula* (fig. 72); the Egyptian warriors of the Exodus wear the uniform of the Roman legionaries (figs. 124 and 127); and Nebuchednezzar is decked out in the *paludamentum* of the Roman emperors (Catacomb of Priscilla). Many figures wear the *tunica manicata*, either loose or gathered in at the waist, and provided with sleeves. History painting, without going to these extremes, made little greater effort to create illusion in this respect.

It will be seen, then, that in the stories taken from the Old Testament the selection shows a choice of increasingly complicated subjects and, slightly later than the Peace of the Church, a marked transition from symbolic meaning to historical narrative, a development parallel on a different plane to what we have already observed in relation to the depiction of Christ.

The New Testament

Under the circumstances it is not very surprising that themes drawn from the New Testament are less numerous during the first period of Early Christian painting. They are fully in evidence but, on the whole, they comprise scenes directly concerned with Christ and his mother, which is why it has seemed natural to group them in this study, in the lists of representations of the former or the latter. Besides, though these themes do not in themselves lack a symbolic sense, they remain directly related to historical actuality and so were not destined to achieve widespread circulation until the Church first came fully into the open. This later development is particularly noticeable in the sixth century, especially at Ravenna in S. Apollinare Nuovo as well as in manuscripts – for example the illuminated manuscript called Rabbula Gospels and, from the same period, the reliefs on the Monza ampullas.

There were some fourth-century representations of episodes from the life of Christ, for example in the New Catacomb of the Via Latina of the soldiers drawing lots for Christ's tunic, and a no longer extant mosaic in the Mausoleum of Constantius showing the centurion kneeling before Christ. It is interesting to notice that certain themes which one might expect to see represented are, in fact, not to be found. This applies to the cycles of Christ's Childhood, Passion and Resurrection (apart from the Adoration of the Magi). According to the rather late evidence of St John Damascene and also the contemporary evidence attributed to St Nilus the Ascetic, these cycles did decorate the Eastern churches, at least, from the fourth century onwards. Various reasons have been advanced for the absence of these themes prior to the fourth century. One which has the support of much scholarly opinion holds that the Early Christians were afraid that the ignominious agony of the crucifixion implied in a representation of Christ might lead pagans to despise their faith. This opinion not only deserves consideration but certainly corresponds at least partially with the truth, in view of the fact that these cycles began to be widely represented from the time of the Peace of the Church onwards. However, this hypothesis does not take into account the absence until the fourth century of two particular cycles, those of Christ's childhood, in general, and of his glorious life. Yet there can have been no reluctance to depict the first aspect, as the figuration of the Virgin Mary since the very beginnings of Early Christian art plainly shows. And if there was reluctance to depict the second aspect, it certainly could not have been because the artists feared an adverse reaction; on the contrary. A detailed study of Early Christian paintings seems to reveal that during the initial period great emphasis was placed upon the symbolic and mystical meaning of the life of Christ and that he was shown in a way that would allow him to be apprehended in the most immediate fashion – that is to say, less through the facts of his life than through his person as foretold specifically in the Old Testament. This interpretation seems to be supported by certain facts which will ultimately emerge from the present classification.

The Apostles

It is not possible to establish as precise a chronology of representations of the Apostles as of representations from the Old Testament. Portraits of Apostles, dating from the third century, adorn the inside walls of the hypogeum of the Aurelians, which also displays a whole row of Apostles side by side, dating from the middle of the third century (fig. 37). In the Catacomb of St Peter and St Marcellinus, the Apostle Peter is shown seated and reading, while a fourth-century painting in the Catacomb of Domitilla presents him standing and holding a book. If we are to attribute the Eucharist depicted (fig. 2) to the third century, then we shall recognize a simpler pattern of the general chronology already established in those categories so far examined.

The Faithful

Full-length and bust portraits are abundant, yet it is not always easy to distinguish representations of the martyrs from those of the other Christians buried in the catacombs, although martyrs must certainly have been the objects of special veneration from the beginning of the Christian era. There can be no doubt in the case of St Thecla depicted at Khargeh in the chapel-mausoleum of the Exodus, attended, according to the most recent interpretation, by seven virgins (fig. 152); the same saint is shown, in the chapel-mausoleum of Peace, with St Paul (fig. 154). But these paintings certainly date from the fourth and fifth centuries. It seems, in fact, that in the catacombs of Rome and elsewhere the iconography of martyrs, as distinct from venerable deceased persons, did not flourish until the beginning of the fourth century. There is still some doubt as to the identity of the six crowned saints of St Sebastian *ad catacumbas* and of a deceased woman in the Catacomb of St Peter and St Marcellinus. But the decoration relating to other deceased figures, some of whom were martyrs, dates from the fourth and fifth centuries. We also know that after the fourth century the catacombs became places of pilgrimage for Christians.

We may thus ascribe the following to the fourth century: the celebrated painting in the Catacomb of Domitilla showing Petronilla, daughter of St Peter, admitting Veneranda into heaven (fig. 31); several subjects in the great ambulatory of the Catacomb of St Januarius in Naples, a group of seven adults, a child with its father and mother, and also two standing adults; in the New Catacomb of the Via Latina a bust of a deceased woman in a circle between garlands and *amorini*, and a standing deceased man in a rectangular frame. To the fifth century belong the three saints, Policamus, Sebastianus and Carinus, figured in the Catacomb of Callixtus, as well as the numerous mosaics at Tabarca in North Africa, set into the lid of the sarcophagus, all depicting figures in *orans* posture standing between flaming torches (figs. 158 and 159).

Symbols

We have already had occasion to mention several times the symbols used by the Christians of the earliest period to interpret adequately the transcendence of Christ's person (for example, by representing him as the Good Shepherd). It must be remembered, in this connection, that this era was generally drawn to symbolism; the tendency is particularly noticeable in pagan funerary art from the second century onwards. If it is true that the Christians inevitably form a part of this whole general movement, it is equally true that they are always distinguishable from their contemporaries by reason of a body of doctrine which gives firmness and consistency to their interpretation of the symbol. In symbolism, the apparent meaning suggests another meaning on a different plane. Anything may serve as a symbol, and the first Christians drew their symbols from many sources: the Old Testament, the New Testament, Jewish writing and iconography, the first Patristic writings, Greek mythology, ancient types of poetry or decoration, types of pagan religion, history, profane themes. Certain symbols may even combine elements from two or more of these categories.

From the Old Testament there emerge not only the personages already mentioned in connection with the Christ figure, such as the Good Shepherd, a symbol used by Christ himself in the Scriptures, but also various popular bucolic themes with which, as has been mentioned, one must associate Orpheus-David. In addition, we find the Lamb, which appears in Isaiah and also in the Apocalypse; the Lamb Multiplying the Bread (Catacomb of Commodilla, fourth century) (fig. 24); the Lamb Haloed between Two Groups of Three Vessels, those of the Miracle at Cana, so that it does, in fact, relate to the New Testament also (originally in the Mausoleum of S. Costanza, turret, fourth century); the Dove featured in the Noah cycle; the Young Goats Drinking at the Fountain, as described in the Psalms (New Catacomb of the Via Latina, fourth century); Moses Striking the Rock, symbolizing Peter through whom Christ makes the fountainhead of blessings gush forth ('gold-glass' base of a drinking vessel in the Vatican, bearing the name of Peter); Susanna as a Lamb between Two Wolves (fig. 55), symbolizing the Lamb-Spirit, thus having two-fold reference to the Old Testament by reason of subject and of symbol (Catacomb of Praetextatus, fourth century); the Heavenly Jerusalem, invoked by the Apocalypse and so following the general line of the New Testament (Hypogeum of the Aurelians, third century); and, in a general manner, the themes borrowed from the Old Testament by the catacomb painters even before the fourth century – Adam and Eve, Noah's Ark, the Sacrifice of Isaac, David Armed with his Sling, the Ascension of Elijah, Daniel in the Lions' Den, the Three Hebrews in the Fiery Furnace, Jonas, Job, Tobias, and so on.

The New Testament – apart from the themes already mentioned: the Good Shepherd, the Lamb, the Miracle at Cana, Heavenly Jerusalem – provided the following themes: the representation of the Wine-Harvesters in connection with the parable of the vineyard in Isaiah, which has some affinity with the Dionysus cycle (Mausoleum of S. Costanza, fourth century) (fig. 135); the Eucharist, whether it be the Apostles with Christ (Catacomb of Callixtus, third century) (fig. 2), or a Young Man Seated at a Table (Catacomb of St Peter and St Marcellinus, fourth century) (fig. 95,) or Two Young Women, Seated, with a Servant Performing a Rite (?) (*ibid*, fourth century); the Good Shepherd Carrying the Lamb-Spirit among his Heavenly Flock of Sheep (Catacomb of Domitilla, fourth century).

As regards paintings – unlike, it seems, mosaics or sarcophagus reliefs – the probability is that the range of Jewish themes contributed not so much symbols as certain scenes with human figures. In addition, several of these scenes appear syncretic with the subjects typical of the Hellenistic era. One may mention, in particular, the sacrifice of Isaac (the synagogue of Dura-Europos), the Paradise with Orpheus Charming the Animals, the Rivers of Paradise, the Seasons and the Zodiac, the Jonah cycle, the Ascension of Elijah in the form of the sun in a chariot drawn by two horses (fig. 119). This last theme, dating from the fifth century, and to be found in the Catacomb of St Peter and St Marcellinus, may be compared with that in the synagogue of Beth Alpha, where he is even surrounded by the signs of the zodiac and of the seasons.

From Patristic literature was taken the symbol of the Tower, reminiscent of that described in Hermas's *The Shepherd* (Catacomb of St Januarius in Naples, third century); and, from the same source of inspiration, no doubt, the Church of the Circumcised and that of the Gentiles (mosaic, S. Sabina, fifth century).

The field of mythology was also fairly thoroughly exploited: Cupid and Psyche (Hypogeum of the Flavians in the Catacomb of Domitilla, third century) (fig. 34); Ulysses and the Sirens (Crypt of Lucina, Catacomb of Callixtus, early third century); the cycle of Hercules, possibly symbolizing strength, in the following episodes: Hercules and Athene Clasping Hands (fig. 105), Hercules Slaying the Hydra (fig. 107), Slaying an Enemy (fig. 108), Picking the Apples in the Garden of the Hesperides (fig. 106), Bringing Back Alcestis from the Lower World (fig. 116), the Death of Admetus Surrounded by his Family (New Catacomb of the Via Latina, fourth century); Demeter Symbolizing Abundance (*ibid*) (fig. 104); *Amorini* in general, which may form part of the Dionysian cycle; finally, through the medium of the Jewish writings, Orpheus (fig. 27) and the Seasons (figs. 47 and 49).

History furnished the tragic death of Cleopatra (New Catacomb of the Via Latina, fourth century). Official iconography provided the subject-matter for the representation of Victory, a winged woman wearing a crown (*ibid*), a Winged Victory (pavement mosaic at Aquileia, fourth century), or the same figure pouring water from a vessel, a syncretism with the New Testament (New Catacomb of the Via Latina, fourth century). Secular reality and Jewish iconography were the sources for the Fish, symbolizing Christ (fig. 11), but also symbolizing the faithful. Ancient literature originated the theme of the Shepherd and his Flock.

The male and female *orans*, symbols of the spirit in prayer, appear to be a pure creation of Christian artists. The first appearance of this figure is on the vault of the crypt of Lucina (Catacomb of Callixtus), dating from the early third century. This particular attitude of prayer is bestowed upon most of the symbolic figures of the Old Testament: Noah (fig. 92), Susanna (fig. 85), Daniel, the Three Hebrews (fig. 79). But, in this respect, mystical meaning tended to assume historical overtones. As an example, a fourth-century painting in the Catacomb of Domitilla shows the matron Veneranda, among flowers symbolizing another world, in an *orans* posture, looking at the martyr Petronilla (fig. 31). The significance is still symbolic, since the martyr Petronilla is admitting the matron Veneranda into Paradise. The *orans* has become an easily identifiable believer. This extension of the original symbolic meaning to a concrete plane is entirely normal. But some confusion is excusable when one sees in the Catacomb of Thraso (fourth century) a large frame displaying a different type of matron, hair dressed in a chignon and covered by a transparent veil which serves only to enhance the elegant arrangement, dressed in a robe ornamented with embroidered bands, dripping with jewellery including some enormous pieces, described by one commentator as 'a portrait of a lady pretending to be an *orans*' and, in fact, that of a woman who was simply praying 'not to have to sacrifice any of the articles of luxury she had enjoyed during her life' (fig. 80).

In this connection, it is also permissible to question the reality of the symbolic meaning attributable to the Hercules cycle (figs. 105–108) or to the subjects of Demeter (fig. 104) and Cleopatra (fig. 110) in the New Catacomb of the Via Latina. It goes without saying that these themes may have been chosen by a pagan member of the family to whom the site belonged. Equally, others may have been depictions of some craft or occupation (see below), but it must not be forgotten that at the beginning of the fourth century a class composed mainly of professional soldiers, some of whom were Christians, gained high positions, and this fact may be reflected in some of the scenes: the bejewelled matron was a social upstart, while the representations of the deceased in the Via Latina Catacomb may simply show admirers of the Labours of Hercules. If these latter were indeed Christians, then their Christian convictions were mingled, no doubt, with an element of expectation that the hoped-for paradise would preserve some of the less spiritual features of the world they lived in.

The difference between allegory and symbol lies, perhaps, in the fact that in the former category the figure itself incorporates no inherent significance but assumes one, either through some attribute assigned to it or simply through an inscription designating it as such. This is very evident at Khargeh, in the chapel-mausoleum called that 'of Peace' (fourth-fifth century), in the case of representations of Justice holding a pair of scales (fig. 155) or of Peace in the form of women and so entitled. The figure of the female *orans* may be considered to stretch the limits of allegory and symbol to their uttermost.

Crafts and Occupations

Some tombs show us persons exercising their craft or occupation, some of whom, as we have already noted, may well have been pagans. In this connection, it is necessary to distinguish between those figures forming part of the composition of a scene from the Old or New Testament or from some mythological cycle on the one hand, and on the other, portraits of the deceased or of martyrs who had, in fact, exercised the calling represented during the course of their lives.

In the first category can be placed the fisherman of the Catacomb of Callixtus (ninth century); the olive-picker (fig. 51) and the harvesters and grape-gatherers of the Catacomb of Praetextatus (third century); two representations of a shepherd, one in bucolic surroundings, in the New Catacomb of the Via Latina (fourth century); the soldiers featured in the crowning with thorns (?) in the Catacomb of Praetextatus (third-fourth century) (fig. 53); the soldiers drawing lots for Christ's tunic (?), in the New Catacomb of the Via Latina (fourth century); the no longer extant mounted centurion of the Mausoleum of S. Costanza (fourth century); serving-men at a banquet in the house of Celius (National Museum, Naples, fourth century); a group of *phalangarii* in the Catacomb Ostrianum (fourth century); a runner holding a stick and accompanied by a dog, in the crypt of the Charioteer in the Catacomb of Maximus (fourth century). To the same category may be added, too, the catacombs' grave-diggers, who belonged to the guild of those who excavated and decorated the catacombs and kept them in good condition, and who are represented on a number of tombs, perhaps as a mark of gratitude on the part of the families concerned, but in any case as part of the general decorative scheme (figs. 1 and 103).

Deceased persons and martyrs are often depicted in the costume and insignia of their craft or occupation, and sometimes in the actual process of exercising it. In this category may be enumerated: an armed soldier in the New Catacomb of the Via Latina (fourth century) (fig. 112); a charioteer with his quadriga, and a group of canephors between two horses, placed along the arching of a crypt, and the same figure's bust portrait between two muses in the lunette of a crypt in the Catacomb of Maximus (fourth century); a group of coopers near two enormous casks, not far from the entrance of the Catacomb of Priscilla (fourth century) (figs. 73 and 74); a group of bakers in a chamber of the Catacomb of Domitilla (fourth century); a naked mariner manning the oars of a ship filled with amphorae of oil and wine, in the Catacomb of Pontianus (fifth century); an athlete holding a javelin in his hand, in St Sebastian *ad catacumbas* (late third century); a medical lecture (?) in the New Catacomb of the Via Latina (fourth century) (fig. 111); a whole series of agricultural scenes (fig. 56), including one showing the martyr giving orders to his steward, in the Hypogeum of Trebius Justus in the Via Latina (fourth century); finally, a humble woman selling vegetables, on an arcosolium of the Catacomb of Callixtus (fourth century) (fig. 10).

Here again it may be observed that human figures with a purely decorative function often date from before the fourth century, whereas people exercising a specific craft or occupation are generally represented as such from the fourth century onwards. Some, like the charioteer and the soldier, display their insignia proudly; others, like the groups of coopers or bakers, prefer to present themselves in the context of a guild. Trebius Justus betrays the typical brashness of the self-made man in flaunting his activities so openly.

Profane Themes

The crafts and occupations represented may also, of course, be classified as profane themes. Other themes may be mentioned at this juncture, most of them decorative – for example, a landscape on the vault of the vestibule of the Flavians in the Catacomb of Domitilla (third century); birds in various catacombs (figs. 13, 28, 50 and 60) and, in mosaic, in an Alexandrine landscape (Mausoleum of S. Costanza, ambulatory, fourth century) (fig. 139); a goat before a pail of milk (vestibule of the Flavians, Catacomb of Domitilla, third century); a group of goats in the cubiculum of Ampliatus in the Catacomb of Domitilla (third century), and a similar group on a ceiling in the Catacomb of St Peter and St Marcellinus (fourth century); finally, a winepress, in mosaic, at Kabr Hiram. It is not absolutely sure whether these subjects did in fact have a connection with the symbolic themes of the Good Shepherd or of the Vineyard.

Decorative Motifs

As has already been mentioned, various decorative motifs served to fill up empty spaces, either at the extremities of vaults and arcosolia, or in the compartments into which the ceilings were divided. Almost all these designs were borrowed from Greco-Roman decorative art. Typical examples are: *amorini* engaged in all manner of picturesque and charming activities (Catacomb of Praetextatus), (figs. 47, 49 and 51), heads derived from ancient masks and reminiscent of those of the paintings at Pompeii or the mosaics at Antioch (the third-century Cappella Graeca in the Catacomb of Priscilla) (fig. 78), acanthus foliage (vestibule of the Flavians, Catacomb of Domitilla, third century), stylized sheaves of corn (New Catacomb of the Via Latina), a peacock in its pride (lunette of the great ambulatory of the Catacomb of St Januarius at Naples, fourth century), a hippocampus (cubiculum of the Catacomb of Domitilla, third century), dolphins (vault of the vestibule of the Flavians, Catacomb of Domitilla, third century), leaping goats (New Catacomb of the Via Latina), antelopes (*ibid*), stylized fountains (*ibid*), caryatides (Mausoleum of S. Costanza; drawing of a no longer existing section dating from the fourth century); finally, the division of ceiling areas into segments radiating from a central point, outlined by thin garlanded lines (cubiculum in the Catacomb of Domitilla, third century, and in the Catacomb of St Januarius in Naples, fourth century), or in geometrical lines (New Catacomb of the Via Latina, fourth century), or in combinations of circles, squares or parallelograms (*ibid* and Mausoleum of S. Costanza, fourth century).

These decorative motifs, both in painting and in mosaic, were used fairly consistently up to and past the end of the fourth century.

Summary

This descriptive catalogue of subjects and motifs shows the existence at the beginning of the fourth century of a well-defined break which was to become accentuated with the advent of the Peace of the Church. The original mysticism which delighted in the symbol's ideal purity, whether its source was Biblical, mythological or historical, gradually assumed a more realistic approach to the subjects taken from the Old and, especially, the New Testament, a development which coincided with the emergence of a new ruling class. This new class went through a phase of displaying artistic evidence of its secular activities, and the resulting works, though treated initially in a style that was occasionally rather vulgar, achieved a measure of refinement while remaining firmly rooted in realism, thus guiding religious decoration towards historical narration.

The Origin of the Choice of Subjects

Faced with such a wide range of subjects, one naturally envisages the existence of an underlying unifying principle. Surely some system of thought must have dictated the choice of subjects in the tomb-paintings of the catacombs, as was the case with the Pharaonic tomb-paintings?

It seems reasonable to suppose that, if one restricts the question to the catacombs alone, the same imperatives which presided over the planning of a new, organized, communal system of burial must equally have governed the elaboration – however unconscious it may have been – of certain rules in decoration capable of translating these new ideas. It would seem clear that such imperatives must be in harmony with the essential aim of the catacombs, which was to preserve the bodies of the dead for the Last Judgement. In terms of Christian doctrine, the main preoccupation was necessarily the salvation of the soul, that being the supreme condition of the blessed resurrection of bodies. The subjects decorating the walls of the catacombs must surely have been chosen as illustrations of this basic concept.

But scholars differ in opinion concerning the manner in which these subjects do in fact illustrate the concept. That great pioneer of catacomb research, the late Mgr. Wilpert, favoured a purely symbolic interpretation of all the scenes, from whatever sources they may have been derived, claiming that the symbol must have been chosen by virtue of its connection with the idea of death. It must be admitted, as we have seen in the previous chapter, that such an opinion contains a measure of truth. In these scenes, either the significance of the symbol is evident or else it is usually emphasized by a detail or even an inscription. This is the case, it will be remembered, with a gilded 'gold-glass' medallion depicting a person striking a rock, where the person in question is not, in fact, described as Moses but carries above it the name of Peter, indicating that the traditional gesture of Moses making the water gush from the rock symbolizes the action of Peter considered as mediator of the Grace whose source is Christ.

But the connection with death, even if it exists, is sometimes rather tenuous. Although it is immediately apparent in the Jonah cycle, which Christ himself mentioned and interpreted in terms of death, it is rather less obvious in scenes showing the Baptism of Christ or the miracle of the Loaves and Fishes. The connection seems even more dubious in the case of the Miracle of the Woman with an Issue of Blood (fig. 99) or of the Adoration of the Magi (fig. 68), not to mention those compositions which show the profession of the deceased man (fig. 73).

In these circumstances, the comparison argued by the supporters of the symbolic interpretation between the scenes from the Old and New Testaments painted in the catacombs and the scenes evoked by the ancient liturgical prayers recited at the bedside of the dying man can by no means be sustained in all cases. Indeed, it is far from being established that these prayers are even contemporary with the catacombs, let alone anterior to them.

Another school of thought, led by Paul Styger, has tried to refute out of hand the purely symbolic interpretation of the catacomb paintings as relating to the idea of death, and claims that each scene represented is to be understood in a purely historical sense, that which it had in the Old or the New Testament. According to this opinion these scenes are more likely to have a bearing on the salvation of the soul in general, but do not refer directly to the theme of death and served simply to foster religious sentiment, as was doubtless their function on the walls of the houses belonging to Christians, where the themes must have been first depicted.

It seems evident that this theory, in attempting to refute the opposing theory, raises more problems than it solves. Apart from ignoring the indisputable symbolism of a large number of scenes, it disregards the evidence of deliberate choice which emerges from the constant repetition of a few of these scenes.

Both views share the failing of taking an over-systematic view of things. There is no doubt that these paintings do have a connection with the idea of death, and necessarily so in view of the general doctrine of the salvation of the soul; but in only a small number of scenes is this connection direct and presented as being an effectual means of salvation, as, for example, in the theme of the Raising of Lazarus. In most other instances, the idea of the salvation of the soul from death is expressed indirectly, in as much as the subject matter may help the soul to keep from or repent from sin and to attach itself to Christ, the saviour of souls, and may, indeed, be open to traditional symbolic interpretations which remain more or less distant from the paintings' most immediate meaning. While denying it any systematic character, one can still assign a limited value to Mgr. Wilpert's idea of linking the choice of scenes in catacomb painting to liturgical prayers.

Even before Paul Styger, Dom Leclerq observed that the 'Prayer for the Recommendation of the Soul' – although it mentions the deliverance of Elijah from death, of Noah from the flood, of Job from his trials, of Isaac from being sacrificed, of Lot from the destruction of Sodom and its inhabitants, of Moses from the Pharaoh, of Daniel from the lions' den, of the Three Hebrews from the fiery furnace, of Susanna from an attempted crime, of David from Goliath, of Thecla from martyrdom – is not to be found in any manuscript anterior to the ninth century, and that even if it goes back to very early Christian times it is still not contemporary with the first catacombs. On the other hand, he compares this prayer with the orisons prescribed by the ancient Jewish liturgy for fast days, pointing out that these orisons contain several of the scenes mentioned in the Christian prayer. He concludes tentatively, but not unreasonably, that there probably exists some kind of link between the prayer and the Jewish fast rituals, a link which may have induced the Christians to choose a certain number of scenes which deal particularly with deliverance from trials and evils.

This idea has been recently renewed and reinforced by the linking up of the scenes in the Dura-Europos synagogue and those in the destroyed church of S. Costanza in Rome with the Jewish and early Christian 'summaries'. These canonical or apocryphal accounts of the glorious deeds of the heroes of the faith and of the miracles performed by God constitute, in the absence of a Jewish iconography earlier than the middle of the third century AD, a particularly interesting fund of literary source material. Common to both Jewish and early Christian communities, these heroic tales guided both categories towards the transformation of these deeds into images which gradually developed into two parallel arts developing subsequently according to their own natural patterns (figs. 165–70 and 131–33).

A similar but rather different approach was once made, based on the facts that, in the third century, Tertullian in his *De Baptismo* elucidates certain baptismal scenes painted in the Chamber of the Sacraments of the Catacomb of Callixtus, and that, out of seven scenes in the Baptistry of Dura-Europos, five reappear in the catacombs: Adam and Eve, David with his Sling, the Good Shepherd, the Good Samaritan, and the Man Stricken with Palsy. In the light of these findings, certain scholars have linked the 'historical' scenes of the New Testament and the symbolic scenes of the Old Testament, not directly with death itself or with the sin which leads to eternal death, but with two categories of writing: first, the primitive catechesis preparatory to the reception of baptism, in so far as it can be deduced from the writings of the ante-Nicene Fathers and, going back further, from the epistles of St Paul and St Peter, the Acts of the Apostles and the Gospels themselves, in which connection it must be remembered that these writings were envisaged as a form of catechism for the instruction of the faithful; secondly, the frequently commentated and statistically well-established recurrence of certain specific catacomb scenes. This catechesis is composed of a series of themes, the oral assimilation of which is necessary to the catechumen before he may receive baptism. These are: the call to salvation and its gratuitousness, faith, the deliverance from sin through divine mercy, the change of life necessary for repentance, salvation by baptismal water, and participation in divine life through the Eucharist. It is known that during the seventh century, contemporaneously with this catechesis, a whole liturgy (many fragments of which survive in the Roman liturgy) was in wide use during Lent and the Paschal period and that readings from the Old and New Testaments were interspersed throughout this liturgy. But most of the scenes contained in these readings correspond to those which recur most frequently in the catacombs. The question remains as to why these particular scenes are so prominent. We have already ruled out the hypothesis of the presence of baptistries in the catacombs, and it is, in any case, unnecessary to reconsider this in the present context. The question can best be answered by assuming that the Christian's faith and hope which accompany the reception of baptism are also the qualities which, firstly, guide the deceased person until the eternal rest which awaits him and, secondly, need to be constantly rekindled in the heart of the faithful.

Other texts, too, group practically the same episodes in different sequences and arrangements. Among those which have most frequently been quoted are a prayer of Cyprian of Antioch (fourth century) which lists the symbols of the efficacity of prayer, and the fourth-century Gelasian Sacramentary which sees in a very similar sequence of scenes the symbols of the spiritual liberation of the catechumen.

There is no reason for surprise at this conclusion: they are, after all, the fundamental symbols of the Christian faith and of its manifestations. In consequence, it seems appropriate to trace the choice of scenes in the catacombs back to their various sources, which may be prayers forming part of the liturgy, or prayers attributable to great saints, or cycles of instruction, such as the catechesis, which lie within the framework of the Christian's essential activities, all these sources having probably been themselves partially nourished at deeper levels which must have formed part of Jewish rituals and 'summaries'.

Although there can be no question of excluding these probable sources, their multiplicity and, because of this multiplicity, their inadequate relevance to the general pattern of the scenes depicted in the catacombs do give rise to a measure of dissatisfaction. Might there not, perhaps, exist a clue which could enable us to link together these various scenes while still taking into account their multiple character?

Furthermore, if it is true that the catacombs form a category apart, the fact remains that the scenes they contain are still interpreted by reference to those which figure in the Dura-Europos baptistry or the Mausoleum of S. Costanza, both of which are constructions of a wholly different nature. How are we to consider these latter paintings or, indeed, all those which decorate the ecclesial house at Dura-Europos or that of Celius in Rome, or those churches which postdate the Peace of the Church? Must one, in fact, make an absolute distinction between catacomb paintings and those decorating other monuments or involving other techniques? The basic question is whether these latter categories do or do not derive from the same sources.

In order to summarize the diverse opinions set out here, and the problems they raise, as well as those which they leave unresolved, one may point out that in the paintings in the catacombs (and elsewhere, sometimes) the symbol is dominant without being exclusive, especially in those scenes dating from the beginning of the Early Christian period; that the allusion to death is direct only in a few cases, such as the Raising of Lazarus, and is even then susceptible of alternative interpretations; that a narrative element is often present and assumes an increasing importance as time goes on, so that from the fifth century onwards at the latest a purely symbolic interpretation is entirely out of the question; that the paintings in the catacombs or other sites give equal prominence, quantitatively, to the themes of baptism and catechism.

There is a solution that seems persuasive in so far as it takes into account not only all the considerations detailed above but also a factor that appears to have been insufficiently considered hitherto: historical evolution. The clue we are seeking might be the concern of the first Christians to imbue their paintings on catacomb walls and other surfaces with the spirit of fundamental Christian faith, that is to say the salvation of the soul by Christ. To obtain this effect the same scenes involve the depiction of the living as much as the dead, and it is natural that these scenes should frequently appear both in the churches, privileged places where the faithful enter into earthly contact with God, and in the catacombs and mausoleums, places in which the faithful achieve a final and lasting contact with God. This very fact ensures that the idea of death can never be wholly absent, but whereas it is predominantly mystical in the earliest Christian times, by the fourth century it has become imbued with more down to earth preoccupations.

The distinction to be made, then, is not necessarily between the paintings on monuments over tombs and the paintings on monuments in places of worship. The real dividing line is to be drawn, it seems, not so much between different sites as between different periods of time. The artistic beginnings were marked by an evident mystical impulse which neglects the concrete circumstances of the evangelical message. In this sense, it carries on the Hebraic message in the form in which it exists, for example, in the Psalms, and also the message which Christ himself was constantly imparting. One need not be surprised at this circumstance when we consider that this whole artistic production was concerned with the journey and with preparation for the journey from the earth to heaven. In any case, the atmosphere of persecution throughout the Empire was calculated to induce a degree of indifference towards terrestrial preoccupations, balanced by an equal degree of reliance in God. And the symbolism which linked the two levels of thought was the most logical point of common reference, especially during this particular era, when the symbol was a constituent part of the thought processes of the time.

But there were periods when the stranglehold of the religious persecution was temporarily relaxed, and the Christian community became suddenly aware of its numerical strength and of its civic importance; under those circumstances, some Christians, obliged to serve as officials or professional soldiers, had to harmonize their mystical yearnings with terrestrial exigencies. So, with the rise of a new class and, with it, of a more commonly accepted conception of reality, a new tendency became apparent: the acceptance of the idea of non-religious figurations, and, sometimes, a concomitant, if innocent, vulgarity. The atmosphere changed and, consequently, the way of approaching pictorial themes, and even the choice of those themes, changed at the same time. This new climate heralded the Christians' integration into life, into society, into a worldly existence. It was destined to remain the normal atmosphere of his life, however much he might regret having, in the ordinary course of events, to sacrifice the symbolic representation of this relationship with God in order to limit himself to a reality which was inevitably exposed to occasional compromises. Yet this new reality was, in some aspects, no less religious, for the impulsion towards mystical meaning was thenceforward to be based on an underlying historical interpretation.

The Artistic Interest of Early Christian Painting

Taking shape, as it did, in a period of transition, Early Christian painting was affected by both advantageous and disadvantageous elements. Chronologically, it fell between two important epochs and was strongly influenced by each in turn. On the one hand there was Roman art, which at the advent of the Christian era had just yielded its finest works, on the other Byzantine art which was destined to monopolize for ten centuries the whole conception of Christian art. During both these periods colour reigned supreme.

It would almost seem as though one should be content to await the emergence of Byzantine art and meanwhile regard Early Christian painting in the West and, partially, in the East as a mere appendage of the final stage of Roman art. And, as we have already pointed out, the Early Christian painting of the East hardly survives to the present day, apart from the works preserved at Dura-Europos, although there are many good reasons for presuming the existence of a Christian art culture in the East during this early period.

Remaining within these limits, and from the simple point of view of the history of art, the fact that the body of work of Early Christian painting during the imperial era belongs within the tradition of Roman pictorial art confers upon it a value which is at least comparable to that of the pagan or secular artistic productions of the same period. One cannot, in effect, study the final manifestations of the pictorial art of Rome without including the evidence of the Early Christian painting of the western world. Although it evolved together with the final stage of Roman painting, Early Christian painting did nevertheless introduce some entirely new elements which helped to precipitate its own separate evolution, and if for a time it remained under the influence of the expiring world of Roman art, it still retained its own personality. There was even a short period, nearly a century before the birth of Byzantine art, when Early Christian painting became the dominant influence. Its themes gradually imposed themselves upon all others, while its inspiration, at least in the West, paralleled that of so-called Roman painting, and partially anticipated the style and colour precepts of Byzantine art. It established itself almost imperceptibly in the West as the successor to Roman painting, while asserting a quite separate identity. For both these reasons, it occupies an essential place in the history of art.

Thus, Early Christian painting in its initial period as much as in its mature period demands consideration from an aesthetic point of view. It is worth examining how, in the West and in certain regions of the East, it forms parts of the final period of Roman painting, and also how and when it freed itself from that influence, ushering in a new era which, even if we restrict ourselves to the evidence of what has survived, can be said to have lasted until medieval times and even beyond.

The stylistic characteristics of the work, as well as certain marks on the bricks supporting the inner walls of the catacombs make it possible to assign the beginnings of Early Christian painting to the first part of the third century. As has already been said, the period of Early Christian painting is held in this study to extend to the end of the fifth century, when Byzantine art was born. Between these limits, however, many uncertainties remain, particularly in the matter of dating. In the absence of positive dates hitherto, we have thought best to follow broadly the exposition of the evolution of painting during this period of art elaborated by the Italian scholar Maurizio Borda in his work *La Pittura Romana* (Milan, 1958).

Decoration

However little one may be interested in Roman painting, one will still recognize at first glance its essential characteristics in the decorative system of the catacomb chambers. What is immediately noticeable is that the decorative motifs in the catacombs are identical with those to be found in the houses of Pompeii and in the Mediterranean mosaics of the first centuries of the Christian era: masks, garlands, dolphins, hippocampi, birds, etc. (figs. 60 and 78). The surfaces of the walls and vaults, and more rarely those of the arcosolia, are divided into compartments by lines, sometimes dentate, of deep colour. On the walls, these lines generally form the outlines of regularly spaced rectangles set side by side, the top lines being slightly concave. Examples of this pattern are to be seen in the Catacomb of Domitilla's hypogeum of the Flavians and in its so-called chamber of David. The walls in the crypt of Ampliatus (early fourth century) are decorated with imitations of architectonic frameworks which serve to give the scenes they frame an illusion of depth, in the manner of the second Pompeiian style.

On the vaults, the arrangement of these lines tends to be less complex. One of the most ancient designs (Catacomb of Callixtus, crypt of Lucina, *c* AD 220) is in the form of a Greek cross combined with a St Andrew's cross radiating from a central medallion and surrounded by a large circle through which the tips of the cross extend. In the Hypogeum of the Aurelians (*c* AD 250), two circles repeat in successive waves the circle surrounding the central medallion; the arms of a simple cross with the medallion as its centre, ending at the line of the first of these surrounding circles, abuts upon lunettes the bases of which conform to the line of the outer second circle. In the Catacomb of St Peter and St Marcellinus (fourth century), the first circle is eliminated and the arms or the cross are so shortened as to form no more than a simple link between the central medallion and the lunettes (chamber of the Good Shepherd); or alternatively, the lunettes themselves are eliminated and the arms of the cross, linked by transversal lines, extend through the available space.

Lines that were originally ornamented with garland patterns soon became quite plain, while the classical decoration of plants, animals or masks also tended to disappear. Simple subjects began to be depicted in the lateral segments of the room walls and, during the course of the first half of the third century, inside the central medallions of the vaults. Complex subjects were reserved for the arcosolia and the central wall-segments; from the fourth century onwards, such subjects also appeared on the vault compartments (Catacomb of St Peter and St Marcellinus).

On the other hand, during the Constantinian era decorative schemes were marked by a refinement of taste and by a certain revival of the classical ideals, exemplified, for example, by the imitation of marble surfaces on panels and the return of naturalistic and elegant motifs. This is the case in the crypt of Eusebius of the Catacomb of Callixtus, in which an arcosolium is decorated by doves surmounted by garlands. This tendency is particularly well illustrated, in a different technique, by the decorative richness of the mosaics in the Mausoleum of S. Costanza; hitherto restricted to flooring, the mosaics here spread to the walls and vaults, taking the place of paintings. The cupola, as we know from sixteenth-century drawings, not only was covered with scenes from the Old and New Testaments and with secular themes but featured three supporting caryatids, each mounted on two felines, a favourite type of ornamentation of the ceilings of Roman houses, notably at Pompeii.

The decoration of the vaults of the ambulatory may, as we have shown, be derived from equally ancient traditional motifs of Italic or Alexandrine origin. The designs – stars formed by combinations of crosses, octagons and elongated hexagons (Vault I), or by crossed rhomboids (Vaults II and XII), and circles in which flowerets alternate with full-length or half-length female figures (Vaults V and IX) – were all anticipated at Pompeii. Other designs are reminiscent of second-century pagan tombs: the octagons formed by enlaced circles and containing flowers, birds and *amorini* (Vaults III and XII) (fig. 134), the wreaths of vines with medallions containing *amorini* and bust portraits, separated by rectangles showing pastoral scenes (Vaults IV and X) (fig. 135). Other designs again are more evocative of an Alexandrine gaiety of imagination: for example, the skilful composition grouping various birds (partridges, peacocks, magpies, hoopoes, etc.) with fruit-laden branches and elegant plates and vessels (Vaults VI and VIII) (fig. 139).

The beginning of the fourth century witnessed a clear break in the decorative style of Christian monuments. The ostentation of the Constantinian period naturally affected the forms of the homage which Christians wished to render to God and his Saints. But there remained a certain liking for the insertion of secular motifs, a tendency which is no longer evident on such monuments from the fifth century onwards. Between the first beginnings of catacomb art and the aesthetic break that occurred at the start of the Constantinian era, a simplicity of outline, which is also to be found in the pagan hypogea of the period, became increasingly evident in the paintings. This new severity may perhaps have been caused by a measure of impoverishment of the painter's craft, which would explain why it is not only the Christian paintings which were affected.

Although the basements of the Christian tombs reflect the same type of ornamentation to be found in pagan tombs, decoration of the vaults, on the other hand, even if it has become simplified, nevertheless shows a genuine inventiveness in the way linear arrangements are contrived. The reason for this may be the number of catacomb tombs being built and the consequent search for decorative variety. This search for variety must be accounted one of the merits of Christian artists in general.

Scenes

Scenes dominated by human figures are to be found in certain types of frame, for example inside the central medallions and the lunettes of the vaults, the same sites inside the arcosolia, and the central panels of the inner walls. It is chiefly through the existence of these figurations that we are able to follow the evolution of iconographic painting during the period in which catacomb art flourished, though we should bear in mind the existence of the third-century decorations of the Dura-Europos house, the fourth- and fifth-century decorations of the mausoleum-chapels of Khargeh in Egypt, the wall-paintings of the fourth-century mausoleums of Centcelles in Spain and S. Costanza in Rome, the fifth-century churches in Palestine, the late fourth-century and early fifth-century Christian monuments of various kinds of North Africa, in addition to the evidence provided by the gold-inlaid bases of drinking vessels.

Three separate periods may be distinguished during this space of time: the first, covering the whole of the third century, inherited the formulas of classical art but initiated a tendency towards abstraction; the second, running from AD 290 to the accession to power of Constantius II, saw the renunciation of naturalism and plastic values in favour of a conventional aesthetic typified by taut outlines; the third, stretching from the reign of Constantius II to the end of the fifth century, marked a return to classicism and plastic values, accompanied by a decorative mannerism, qualities balanced eventually by a renewed hieratic style. And from the second third of the fourth century onwards, mosaic work began to encroach upon the preserves of wall-painting, finally taking over completely for a long period of time, except in certain parts of Italy, notably Rome and Milan.

The third century was, in the present context, a period of indecision, during which the predominant influence of classical painting was gradually affected by new though still relatively hesitant conceptions. The classical manner inherited from the Antonines is already apparent in AD 220 in the Catacomb of Callixtus and is to be found again a few years later in, for example, the Catacomb of Priscilla. In both the vault of the crypt of Lucina in the first-mentioned edifice (fig. 12), and in a particular chamber in the second (fig. 71), paintings of the Good Shepherd share a quality of harmony that allies minuteness of detail to an apparent absence of effort; the naturalness and elegance of Christ's posture, the finely moulded symmetry of the two lambs and the plant-life forming the background all demonstrate a self-confident awareness on the part of the artist. In the Catacomb of Callixtus, too, in the gallery of the Sacraments, the symbolic image (from the Eucharist) of the Fish surmounted by a basket containing bread and wine is depicted in outlines which are both precise yet graceful (fig. 11).

But during more or less this same period of time, a different style became evident almost everywhere, a style that substituted sketched strokes for precise outline and minuteness of detail, illusionism for naturalism and vivid gestures for elegant attitudes; a style that no longer allowed the observer to gaze in tranquil and satisfied contemplation, but required him to withdraw to a certain distance in order to follow the movement in proper perspective. This is exemplified in the episode of the Woman of Samaria (fig. 4) depicted in the Catacomb of Callixtus, and, despite the classical poses, in the theme of the Virgin with Balaam showing her the star in the Catacomb of Priscilla (fig. 67).

These rival styles were both firmly established by about AD 240 and neither was entirely abandoned during the era of Early Christian painting. In the Catacomb of Priscilla, for example, in the chamber of the Velatio, the figures depicted on the back wall (fig. 69) are classical in concept, whereas in the Hypogeum of the Aurelians a sort of impressionism emerges from the scene of the shepherd reading a book near his lambs (fig. 36). But at the same time a popular reaction in favour of realism is evident in the very same hypogeum, in the third chamber, in the scene of the rider (perhaps the Antichrist) arriving from the city surrounded by young people, and in the portraits of intense-faced Apostles (fig. 37).

It is of some interest to observe that at that very moment (AD 232–3) exactly similar hesitation between styles manifested itself somewhat beyond the farther end of the Mediterranean, at Dura-Europos: in the ecclesial house, the Good Shepherd, here an ephebe but with a stance that is both free and majestic, contrasts with a group comprising a stiffly composed Adam and Eve; and in the baptistry, for example, the realism and sureness of feeling that mark the scene of Christ on the lake holding his hand out to Peter are equally in contrast with the slow rhythm of the three torchbearing Marys, the centre one seen in full face while the other two face her from each side. At the same site, the temple of Zeus Theos, which antedates the ecclesial house, and the synagogue (fig. 170), both contain several narrative paintings that give clear evidence of the continuing influence of Roman art precepts, although occasionally a purely Eastern hieratic element intrudes.

During the second half of the third century, there appears to have been a process of oscillation and, occasionally, these opposite tendencies tended to blend. For example, in the Catacomb of Domitilla's Hypogeum of the Flavians, the famous but unfortunately very damaged scene of Eros and Psyche (fig. 34) is conspicuous for its naturalism and gracefulness, yet the Psyche is, in fact, essentially impressionistic in outline; again, in the Catacomb of St Peter and St Marcellinus, the slightly later composition depicting the celestial banquet of Agape and Irene (fig. 89), though classical in conception, gives a fluidity to the figures which contrasts with the traditional modelling. Yet at approximately the same time (AD 270–75) the painting in the *Coemeterium Maius* depicting a female *orans* and two shepherds gives a hard, dry outline to the figures involved which contrasts strangely with the classical and vivid idiom of the main composition (fig. 20).

During the third century, a similar development occurred in pagan painting, and this evolution is to be seen, for example, in Ostia, as well as in some pre-Constantinian tombs in the Vatican, and in one of the hypogea of Maghara el Djedida. But in comparison, the catacomb paintings are aesthetically superior, and some of these remain supreme, especially the scenes of the Good Shepherd in the Catacombs of Callixtus (fig. 12) and Priscilla (fig. 71), and the scene of Mary with Balaam (fig. 67). Other catacomb paintings, such as the scene of the Crowning with Thorns (?) in the Catacomb of Praetextatus (fig. 53), must be accounted of inferior interest aesthetically and, as we have seen, many paintings show a hesitation between conflicting styles; but, on the whole, most catacomb paintings demonstrate a stylistic balance between these styles, as exemplified by the scene of Eros and Psyche in the Hypogeum of the Flavians (fig. 34), by the chamber of the Velatio in the Catacomb of Priscilla (fig. 69), and, even, that of the female *orans* between two shepherds in the *Coemeterium Maius* (fig. 20).

This balance was destroyed around AD 290, by which date Diocletian had established the First Tetrarchy in order to safeguard his regime against the hazards of military coups, and had moved his capital eastwards in response to the increasing pressure from that quarter. Society became transformed in the interests of a military class with simpler and coarser tastes. This political upheaval was accompanied by a new aesthetic perspective, involving the renunciation of naturalism: volumetric forms either fill out through bunching or, on the contrary, become angular and inorganic. When modelling is in evidence at all, it is obtained by *chiaroscuro* (contrasts of light and shadow). During the reign of Constantine, this tendency was to become accentuated by a progressive abandonment of plastic values in the treatment of faces and bodies and by the adoption of an almost conventional aesthetic.

The Catacomb of St Peter and St Marcellinus, dating from the end of the third century, offers numerous illustrations of this change of perspective. In a scene of a celestial banquet the forms are geometric and stiff, while in a scene of Moses Striking the Rock (fig. 96), the forms are bunched and filled out, and in the Adam and Eve group the use of *chiaroscuro* is very evident (fig. 98). The Catacomb of the Jordani contains, in its fourth chapel, a scene of Christ among the Apostles (fig. 43), which is considered to be the first known example of the new manner: in any case, the figures are dry and conventional.

These tendencies become syncretized during the Constantinian era. A new approach was favoured for a time, involving an expression of abstraction and expressionism at the expense of depth, plasticity and proportion, and invoking new themes. Mythological and classical subjects are abandoned or lose their significance almost entirely. Thenceforward the predominant themes are those which had previously been confined to the catacombs and certainly, too, to the ecclesial houses, together with those new formulations which were appropriate to a developing Church eager to make use of the realities of the time, especially their newly-won official power, to translate more effectively the realities announced in its dogmas. As a result of the abandonment of ancient literary themes and the rise of a new class, popular subjects which bordered on the profane began to be introduced. Although it may be said that a new era was opened by the coming to power of Constantine and the Church's consequent emergence into the open, this is true mainly because of the sudden huge accession of Christian themes. A style established itself on the basis of this new fact, but it was limited to marking a particular transitional point in relation to the previous style.

In the Catacomb of Callixtus, arcosolium of Abraham, a scene of the Resurrection of Abraham (AD 340) clearly shows the abandonment of plastic values: the face has become spheroid and expressionless. The same change is to be seen in numerous 'gold-glass' bases, such as that in the Catacomb of Pamphilus depicting the Multiplication of the Loaves and Fishes. A certain hieratic quality affects these figures, as it does the representation of the Virgin in the *Coemeterium Maius* near the crypt of St Emerentiana, where her gaze is intense and her hair arrangement looks like that of a court lady (fig. 14). The female figures in the *orans* attitude depicted in the murals of the Catacomb of Thraso (fig. 80) are also depicted in the new manner, although, as previously noted, the richness of their accoutrements seems inappropriate. And during the same epoch, a scene depicted in the Hypogeum of Trebius Justus sets out pretentiously and more or less in popular fashion the proprietor's functions as a great landowner and housebuilder (fig. 56).

With Constantius II, there opened a new and final period which was to encompass the remaining years of the fourth century and the whole of the fifth century, covering the reigns of Julian the Apostate (361–3), Valentinian I (364–75), Theodosius (379–95), Honorius (395–423), and going beyond that. In fact, the reign of Constantius II saw a partial return to classicism: clearly defined contours are to be observed, for example, in the symbolic representation of Susanna as an ewe-lamb between two wolves (fig. 55), to be found in the Catacomb of Praetextatus, and certainly in the paintings in the New Catacomb of the Via Latina. The mosaics in the Mausoleum of S. Costanza also date from this period; apart from the naturalistic or geometric decorations of the vaults in the ambulatory (figs. 134 and 139), these mosaics also feature wine-harvesting (fig. 135) and pastoral scenes which, while their aim is evangelical, are nevertheless treated in classical fashion, except that the human figures and the animals show the squat outlines characteristic of the preceding period.

Now plastic values are reintroduced. In the Catacomb of Callixtus, the crypt of the Lambs, a scene of Moses Striking the Rock (fig. 8) presents human figures who once again have flesh on their bones. Later that century, during the reign of Valentinian I, the crypt of St Petronilla and St Veneranda (fig. 31) near the basilica of St Nereus and St Achilles in the Catacomb of Domitilla exhibits well-constructed, elegantly draped figures who are modelled in a classic style. The *Maiestas Domini* not only shows this new tendency clearly but may well have initiated it. The divine face is delineated with precisely outlined, almost naturalistic strokes in a portrait to be seen on the ceiling of the Catacomb of Commodilla (fig. 22). In the Catacomb of St Peter and St Marcellinus, the Saviour holding the Gospel Book sits enthroned between Peter and Paul above the Lamb, which is standing upon a mound flanked by four martyrs (fig. 90), a scene that recalls those to be found in the Mausoleum of S. Costanza (figs. 136 and 137).

Profane subjects not only adjoin Christian subjects, even on the sarco-phagi, but greatly outnumber the latter, in terms of surviving examples. This we have seen to be true of the mosaics of the Mausoleum of S. Costanza. It is equally true of the crypt of Ampliatus in the Catacomb of Domitilla, in which the landscape is depicted more or less for its own sake; in the latter instance, the effect is almost one of a return to *trompe l'oeil* architecture.

During the fifth century, paintings continued to be executed in the catacombs, though in a period when pilgrimages to the tombs of the first Christians were just starting, these paintings were made for the benefit of the living as much as the dead. Nevertheless, technique deteri-orated considerably, and themes tended to be repeated interminably. Only a very few scenes hold the attention: for example, the seafaring man in the Catacomb of St Pontianus, or Peter with a child in the Cata-comb of St Gaudiosus in Naples. Mosaic work came to the fore, but avoided the profane and classicizing tendencies that affected mid-fourth-century art.

In this manner, composition adopted a more hieratic rhythm; standing figures are placed inside large rectangular frames, in scenes which some-times cover considerable surfaces. At the same time, the technique de-teriorates, and outlines are apparently hastily sketched. A popular vein is to be detected in the decoration of the Roman catacombs (especially those dating from the fifth century) which had already been anticipated in the third century. A corresponding trend is to be seen in North Afri-can mosaic work, where funerary slabs near Kelibia, dating from the late fifth century, feature birds and plant-life in the decorative scheme around the legend, designed in a style that is still classical in conception. On the other hand, during the late fourth and early fifth century, funerary urns at Tabarca show *orans* figures depicted full-face, in rigid attitudes and drawn in a very primitive manner (figs. 158, 159 and 160).

Similarly, a marked contrast is to be noticed between the *Maiestas Do-mini* in the Catacomb of Domitilla, section of the Great Apostles, or the same theme in the *Coemeterium Maius*, dating from the late fourth cen-tury, on the one side, and, on the other, the restored apsidal mosaic in the Church of S. Pudentiana, in which the Christ figure is enthroned among disciples striking various poses against a background symbolizing Jeru-salem, depicted in vibrant sky-blue shades of colour. This contrast em-phasizes the arrival of a new approach directly inspired by Court art.

This latter tendency established a synthesis between hieratic art, remnants of Roman influence and provincial traits, a mixture of influ-ences which is visible in the mosaics from the Great Palace at Constanti-nople (figs. 145 to 148), in those recently discovered in the founda-tions of the present Town Hall of Constantinople (figs. 149 and 150), and also, with different nuances, in the two Virgil manuscripts in the Vatican Library (figs. 172 to 175).

In any case, the Church paralleled the patronage bestowed by the Palace on profane art by sponsoring decorative work in general, and religious painting in particular. Having funds from the imperial treasury at its disposal, the Church was able not only to dictate a choice of more or less didactic themes but also to have the best artists of the period work on the elaboration of these themes. Manuscript illumination was encouraged actively by the Church, as is proved by a translation of the Book of Kings whose few surviving leaves, called the *Itala* manuscript, are in Berlin. But the new interest of the Church in the arts served, above all, to encourage the extremely costly medium of mosaic, so that mosaic work now became a more important decorative medium than ordinary wall-painting.

The towns of imperial Italy began to glow with the rich colours of the newly-created mosaic work. In Ravenna, in the Mausoleum of Galla Placidia (fig. 142), in the baptistry called 'of the orthodox', the scenes are full of a sense of airiness, and the carefully posed figures are draped in the classical manner. At S. Maria Maggiore, on the other hand, similar groups are pressed closely together to achieve the desired effect (fig. 176). These mosaics initiate the historical cycles. Backgrounds of landscapes and panoramas remain predominant, and so provide a link with classical antiquity, as does an element of plasticity in the human figures, obtained by the use of shaded contours. These characteristics were to disappear with the hieratic tendencies of eastern origin that asserted themselves during the following century, but the instructional narrative cycles, the major themes such as the *Maiestas Domini* and the *Traditio Legis*, and even the technique of mosaic work already formed part of Byzantine art.

Is There a Specifically Christian Art?

The beginnings of Early Christian painting were, as we have seen, bound up partially with Roman painting, but even at that primary stage it was quite capable of preserving its separate identity, and later it progressively took over the initiative from Roman art while asserting new ways of thought and new themes; so there can be no doubt that it constitutes a well-defined entity in the history of art, possessing its own characteristics and its own evolution. That Early Christian painting was able to detach itself gradually and subtly from Roman painting without actually breaking with it, and was able to continue under its own impetus while taking advantage of the new conditions resulting from the Peace of the Church, is a fact sufficient to endow it with a profound originality which might be considered merit enough without further consideration. Yet it would perhaps be of interest to add a fresh perspective by considering what was the essentially personal factor involved, since this might explain how it was able to formulate its identity through contact with another already established art form, then to develop according to its own natural pattern. In short, while we have hitherto presented Early Christian painting as the testimony of the art of an epoch, do we also possess enough evidence to see in it the testimony of a specifically Christian art?

An examination of the question might well persuade one of the existence in Early Christian painting of a specifically Christian art, but the arguments in favour of this opinion are not mandatory. In the bucolic and decorative themes which they borrowed from mythology, the Early Christian artists exercised a certain choice, retaining in general only those scenes the elements of which approximated to Biblical visions or Christian concepts or at least did not conflict with them – such themes as that of the Good Shepherd, and the pastoral scenes, Eros and Psyche, the Dolphin, and so on.

New themes of Biblical and Christian origin were also introduced, some of which, such as the *orans* and the Virgin, were more or less fresh creations. In the beginning these themes paralleled those depicted on pagan tombs and monuments and later probably outnumbered them, while by the time the Peace of the Church had been established they had eliminated the pagan themes almost entirely. During this last period, Roman painting was in the process of becoming, at least in the religious field, a painting of Christian iconography. Most of the old aristocracy of Rome remained pagan for another century and its members continued to decorate their houses with paintings reflecting their beliefs; there is no lack of examples of pagan decorative schemes such as, for example, the mosaics of the Piazza Armerina in Sicily (figs. 156 and 157). But Christianity became an increasingly powerful influence in the Court and among the new ruling classes: from that time onwards, the great religious constructions were all of Christian inspiration, and the influence of Christianity extended itself even to secular monuments and non-religious objects of clothing and furniture.

However, the replacement of one group of themes by another does not in itself allow one to postulate the transformation of one art into another. A new art requires its own style, the elaboration of which devolves entirely upon it, and whatever the themes in use may be this is the essential precondition of its existence. But such is not the case here. Christianity was only one force among others in the break with classical style and the formation of a new style, even though it was of prime importance and became finally the only important influence. Although the themes in use from the time of Constantine onwards became Christian to a great extent, the style remained typical of the period, and though this style did correspond to the Christian vision of things, Christianity did not create the style and can make no claim to be its sole begetter. Indeed, Early

Christian painting might well be described as Roman painting baptized.

We may ask ourselves, nevertheless, whether Early Christian painting contains some essential quality of Christian vision, and whether in this general transformation of art Early Christian painting may be distinguished by characteristics peculiar to it. Here, the answer is in the affirmative. Already, the choice of themes indicates a very positive vision which swept aside the frequently licentious side of Greco-Roman mythology while still retaining the values of universally human significance, such as love, and placing them on a mystical plane worthy of their divine nature (fig. 34). And an important contribution to this whole new look at things was made by the invention of new themes such as the *orans* (fig. 69) and the Virgin (fig. 68), and by the original combinations of themes from the Old and New Testaments such as the subject of the Virgin with Balaam (fig. 67).

During the pre-Constantinian period, this new look often consisted of no more than a single detail capable of evoking a whole scene: this is so in the case of the Man Stricken with Palsy, shown carrying his bed, while the Christ who had just healed him is not represented, or in the case of Noah shown rising out of a square receptacle (fig. 92). Early Christian painting is still permeated by the general style typical of the period, but except in the very earliest phase landscape and architecture are eliminated to allow greater prominence to the subject's essential elements, so that although the central characters are no doubt meant to be standing on one ideal line, they give every appearance of being already in another world. But this tendency changes during the Constantinian period. The restraint and even bareness that seemed designed to emphasize the underlying idea at the expense of explicit content now give way to inventiveness and gracefulness, as in many of the halls of the New Catacomb of the Via Latina (fig. 119), and acquire a whole range of architectonic embellishment (same catacomb, Raising of Lazarus) (fig. 117), and vividness (Mausoleum of S. Costanza) (fig. 135). The new approach seems characterized by a sort of explosion of joy, a new symbolism in which the whole of nature participates in the work of salvation.

In fact, this new look at things transcends immediate reality and, as a result, though firmly based in contemporary preoccupations it carefully preserves its own identity, going far beyond the vision of Roman painting while helping to hasten the latter's evolution. This process affected not only symbolic figures but equally the scenes drawn from the Old and New Testaments, which were gradually blended into new scenes, the scope of which reaches beyond the human plane to attain the Christian plane without abandoning the former. There results a body of painting which cannot fail to strike one as being entirely original when compared with work of pagan inspiration.

Early Christian painting was, in fact, in the position of being able to borrow graphic, scenic and compositional features with impunity from classical art, or to inherit from a new climate of expression a fluid line, contrasted surfaces or a hieratic appearance; it was necessarily the continuing agent on the Christian plane of the pagan funerary art which had been deeply influenced by symbolism from the second century onwards; it was even capable of passing, in its own evolution, from the symbolic view predominant during the third century to the historical narrative manner of the fourth century (fig. 124), and, especially, of the fifth century. At the same time, the Christian vision directed towards a clearly defined mystical extra-terrestrial world contrasted with the inconsistency of contemporary viewpoints, which were particularly at variance in the matter of the interpretation of symbols. The result was a unity of expression compounded of a particular choice of subjects, a calmness of composition, and a rather ethereal aura emanating from the figures involved.

These elements created an orientation that was to be typical of Early Christian painting from its beginnings in the catacombs when pagan painting was still flourishing up to the moment when pagan art finally expired. If a Christian style exists it is to be found in this combination of elements, reinforced by its religious inspiration. Early Christian painting may thus be considered to possess certain unique features while still remaining attached to a local and historical context. In point of fact, its development is entirely compatible with the logic of Christianity, which teaches that man, while remaining what he is, is made for things higher than himself. Early Christian painting conveys this feeling admirably and may, in this respect, be considered to be a true product of Christian inspiration and so, if one wishes to put it that way, the expression of a Christian art.

Social Evidence

As we have seen, the predominant feature of catacomb painting is its symbolic significance, the intention evidently being to capture an essentially spiritual reality or at least to show a way to its realization. Symbolism provides the medium through which these paintings and pictorial scenes are able to call into play an inner eye operating on an extra-sensual plane. Involved, as one is, in an atmosphere which demands silence above all, one can hardly fail to recall Christ's statement that while the Christian is not *of* the world, he is certainly *in* the world. It might be said, and this would be an added point in support of the principle of a specifically Christian art, that the independence of the Christian in relation to the world has perhaps never been more effectively demonstrated. The degrees and means of this independence are of some interest since, to the extent that they are analysable, they do give us valid information about the religious life of Christians.

If he was not of the world, the Early Christian was in the world, and whatever effort he might make to set the world at a distance, he ended up by taking it with him. In the catacombs and sometimes in the ecclesial houses where he tried to escape the world, just as much as in the churches where he no longer had any reason to feel a fugitive, he combined the visible forces and directed them towards God, remaining meanwhile a witness of his own time.

These two aspects constitute separate funds of documentation, which deserve to be taken into consideration if one wishes to understand the motivating features of Early Christian painting.

Restricting ourselves inevitably to the manifestations of Early Christian painting in the West, and regarding the subject from a point of view slightly different from that with which we studied the question of themes, we may be in a position to draw some tentative conclusions about the social circles to which the Christians belonged at the time.

The catacomb paintings provide no information whatsoever about the Roman aristocracy. As we have remarked, the hypogea around and under which the catacombs grew did not necessarily provide their kernel, and we cannot even be sure that the noble families who were their owners did, in fact, include Christians among their members. Nevertheless, for the Christian faith to have penetrated as it did the social circles in which Constantine moved at the end of the third century, it is evident that the Imperial court must have included a certain number of Christians throughout the period preceding the Peace of the Church and even while the persecutions were raging. It is significant, however, that very few of these socially distinguished believers, if any at all, appear to have sought to have their likenesses depicted in the catacombs, while no evidence has been found to suggest that anyone thought of having this done on their behalf.

But this fact, characteristic of genuine nobility, contrasts with the pretentions of the vulgar rich which we have already remarked upon in connection with the fourth century, Trebius Justus (fig. 56) and the Matrons (fig. 80). The liberal professions, too, waited until the fourth century, it seems, before allowing themselves to figure on paintings. This applies to the physician (?) portrayed in the New Catacomb of the Via Latina, as also to the charioteer of the Catacomb of Maximus in the Via Salaria Nuovo, and the athlete in St Sebastian *ad catacumbas*.

Whether these wall-paintings are meant to show occupations actually exercised by Christians buried in the catacombs, or rather occupations introduced to identify particular characters in Old or New Testament scenes, the social categories represented are in both cases those of the peasantry, the military, merchants and artisans, a fact showing the closer contact with everyday life which became possible, for both artists and simple believers, from the fourth century onwards.

The world of the peasant may be held to embrace all the subjects dealing with one or another aspect of husbandry, and some of the scenes depicted include: Shepherds with their Flocks, as in the New Catacomb of the Via Latina; a Group of Goats, as in the chamber of Ampliatus, Catacomb of Domitilla; the Goat before a Pail of Milk in the Hypogeum of the Flavians in the same catacomb; the Olive-Picker appropriately outlined against a Roman countryside, as in the crypt of St Januarius in the Catacomb of Praetextatus (figs. 47 and 51); Farmers and Wine-Harvesters in the Mausoleum of S. Costanza (fig. 135); the similar scene of the Wine-Press in Kabr Hiram; and the Fisherman in the Catacomb of Callixtus (fig. 9).

Among the representations of military men, only one, in the Church of S. Costanza, shows a soldier of the rank of centurion, and he appears in the context of a scene from the Scriptures; the other examples are all of common soldiers and relate either to the Crowning with Thorns (?), as in the Catacomb of Praetextatus (fig. 53), or to the Drawing by Lot for Christ's Tunic (?), as in the New Catacomb of the Via Latina.

The merchant class is represented notably by the mariner with a ship carrying a cargo of large jars, in the Catacomb of Pontianus, and by the female vegetable hawker in the Catacomb of Callixtus (fig. 10).

The artisans are either connected with general agricultural activities, as for example the coopers in the Catacomb of Priscilla (figs. 73 and 74) or even the bakers in the Catacomb of Domitilla, or else they represent workmen directly involved in the building and maintenance of the catacombs, such as the grave-diggers who appear so frequently (figs. 1 and 103).

The choice of subjects casts some light upon the Christian's social origins. The massive borrowings from the Old Testament imply – at least in the earliest period – either the conversion of numerous Jews as a result of the apostles' application of the Gospel's policy of addressing initially the people of the Covenant, or alternatively a religious culture in direct contact with the Bible through actual reading of the Scriptures or, more probably, by listening to the preaching of those nurtured on the Gospel's teaching.

It has been pointed out by previous authorities that the Gospel of St John among all others provides the source for the greatest number of the scenes from the Scriptures reproduced in the catacombs. These scenes include the Good Shepherd, the Raising of Lazarus, the story of Jonah, the Multiplication of Loaves and Fishes, the Woman of Samaria, the Infirm Man by the Bethesda pool, the Marriage at Cana, the Miracle of the

Man Blind from Birth. This predominant influence is doubtless due, at least in part, to the fact that this Apostle lived to a very old age, and to his authority as a direct witness of Christ through the many years of their association, factors which more than compensate for his physical distance from the Roman scene.

The conclusions which emerge naturally from this analysis of the subjects represented are its most interesting aspect. The piety of the first Christians, however steeped it may have been in Old Testament lore, was, as we might expect, essentially Christological in nature. But during the whole period preceding the Peace of the Church, that is to say so long as the Christians were unable to participate with full freedom in the city's social life and obligations, this piety remained centred upon the purely symbolic aspect of the subjects represented, a symbolism that was intended to give direct access to the work of salvation and the beyond, but brushed aside the same symbol's profane or historical significance.

On the other hand, this gradually acquired liberty enabled certain Christians, in all innocence perhaps, to derive from the world a few of its advantages of wealth and dignity; in any case this liberty provided the basis for historical rather than uniquely symbolic representations, the subjects of which are involved in the life of the world without, however, sacrificing any element of the mystery. The two extreme attitudes – symbolism and historical narrative – are both equally acceptable to the essential tenets of the Christian doctrine, based as they are on the concept of Incarnation. These attitudes are evidence of the richness of religious life in this Early Christian period, and of the religious inspiration that lay behind its painting – perhaps the most important single aspect of Early Christian art – and constitute in themselves the best conclusion, probably, to be drawn from this general survey of the subject.

Conclusion

Early Christian painting may be considered an entirety in which, in the West, an evolution is easily perceptible, impelled partly by the forces inherent in Roman painting and partly by outside influences, especially some coming from the East, but among which the Christian faith must be considered super-eminent.

Though it may be true that most of the surviving examples of Early Christian painting represent a prolongation of Roman art with the added grace of Baptism, it still remains an original art based on religious inspiration, and in this respect it resembles several other periods of art and is equally precise in its structure.

The general body of work produced by Early Christian art allows us to come to some profound conclusions about the categories to which the first Christians belonged and about Roman society in general. In the West, at least, it reflects the social evolutions of the time and, above all, the change of religious perspective within the context of Christianity's essential precepts, which followed upon the conversion of Constantine and the subsequent Peace of the Church.

Although the Constantinian era witnessed the more direct involvement of Christian life with the everyday world, the manifestations of its art remained deeply affected by the mystical atmosphere that surrounded its beginnings. Most important of all, it furnishes the art historian with the base upon which all Christian art rests, its themes, its mental outlook and even its style. During the two eras into which it is divided – the line of separation being traceable in the early part of the fourth century – it offers the two aspects between which all Christian art will always fluctuate, according to whether its aim is to reach towards the invisible through the medium of the visible, or to reveal the eternal in history.

Bibliography

R. Bianchi-Bandinelli, 'Continuita ellenistica nella pittura de eta medio e tar-do-romano', in: *Riv. dell' Instituto Nazionale d'Archeologia e Storia dell' Arte*, 1953, p. 1–85

Mgr. L. de Bruyne, 'Les "lois" de l'art paléochrétien comme instrument hermé-neutique', in: *Riv. di Arch. cristiana, XXXV*, 1959, p. 105–186

C. Cechelli, *I Mosaica della Basilica di Santa Maria Maggiore*. Turin, 1956

E. Coche de la Ferte, 'Art paléochrétien', in: *Histoire Générale de L'Art*, vol. II, *(Encyclopédie de la Pléiade)*. Paris

J. Danielou, *Les symboles chrétiens primitifs*. Paris, 1961

N. Duval, 'Deux basiliques chrétiennes de Tunisie méridionale', in: *Cahiers archéologiques, XI*, 1960, p. 41–61

The Excavations at Dura-Europos, Final Report, Part I. New Haven, 1956

A. Ferrua, *Le Pittura della nuova catacomba di Via Latina*. Rome, 1960

P. A. Fevrier, 'Études sur les catacombes romaines', in: *Cahiers archéologiques, X*, 1959, *XI*, 1960

J. B. Frey, 'Il delfino col tridente nella Catacomba Giudaica di Via Nomentana', in: *Riv. di Arch. crist., VIII*, 1931, p. 307–314

E. R. Goodenough, *Jewish Symbols in the Greco-Roman Period* (Bollingen Foundation). New York, 1958, 2 vols.

A. Grabar, *La Peinture byzantine*. Geneva: Skira, 1953

A. Grabar, 'Recherches sur les sources juives de l'art paléochrétien', in: *Cahiers archéologiques, XI*, 1960, p. 41–61

A. Grabar et C. Nordenfalk, *Le Haut Moyen-Age*. Geneva: Skira, 1957

F. Josi, 'Coemeterium majus', in: *Riv. de Arch. crist., X*, 1933, p. 7–16

F. Josi, 'Le pitture rinvenute nel cimiterio dei Giordani', *ibid., V*, 1928, p. 167-227

G. P. Kirsch, 'Un gruppo di cripte dipinte inedite del Cimiterio dei SS. Pietro e Marcellino', *ibid., VII*, 1930, p. 203–234

F. Kirschbaum, *The Roman Catacombs and Their Martyrs*. New York: The Bruce Publishing Company, 1956

Dom H. Leclerq, *Manuel d'Archéologie chrétienne*. Paris, 1907, 2 vols.

A. G. Martimort, 'L'iconographie des Catacombes et la catéchèse antique', in: *Riv. di Arch. crist., XXV*, 1949, p. 106–114

B. Pace, *I Mosaici di Piazza Armerina*. Rome, 1955

G. Ch. Picard, 'Mosaici greci e romani', in: *Encyclopedia universale dell' arte*, Venice, Rome, 1963, col. 676–683, article on Mosaics.

A. M. Schneider, *Die Brotvermehrungskirche von et-Tabgah am Genesareth und ihre Mosaiken*. Paderborn, 1934

H. Stern, 'Les Mosaïques de L'Église Sainte Constance à Rome', in: *Dumbarton Oaks Papers 12*, 1958, p. 157–218

H. Stern, 'Quelques problèmes d'iconographie paléochrétienne et juive', in *Cahiers archéologiques, XII*, 1962, p. 99–113

P. Styger, *Die Romischen Katacumben*. Berlin, 1933

D. Talbot Rice, *The Beginnings of Christian Art*. London, 1957

D. Talbot Rice, *The Great Palace of the Byzantine Emperors*, second report: 'The Mosaics'. University of St Andrews, Edinburgh, 1959

G. Ville, 'La Mosaïque antique', in: *L'Information d'histoire de l'art, 1961*, no. 3, p. 61–71

Mgr. J. Wilpert, *Die römischen Mosaiken und Malereien der kirchlichen Bauten von IV bis zum XIII Jahrhundert*. Freiburg. 1916

Mgr. J. Wilpert, *Pittura delle catacombe romane*. Rome, 1903

Early Christian Painting

Illustrations

1

2

4

7

8

9

14

17

18

19

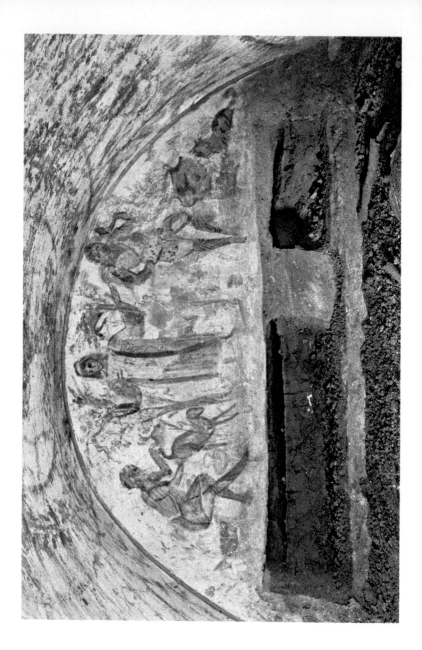

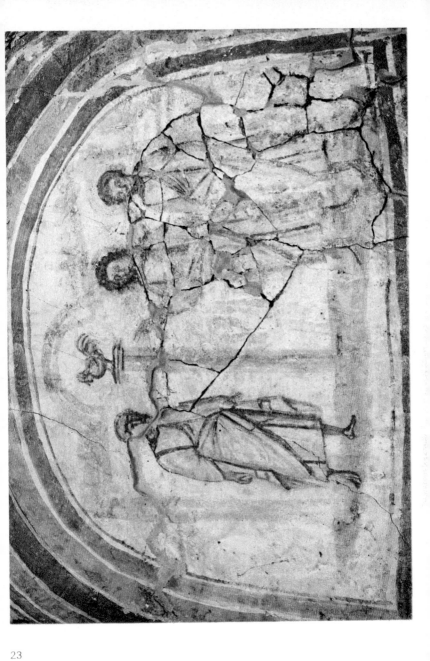

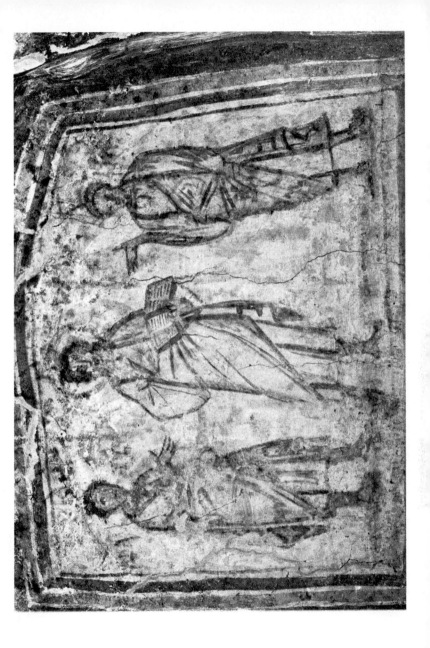

25

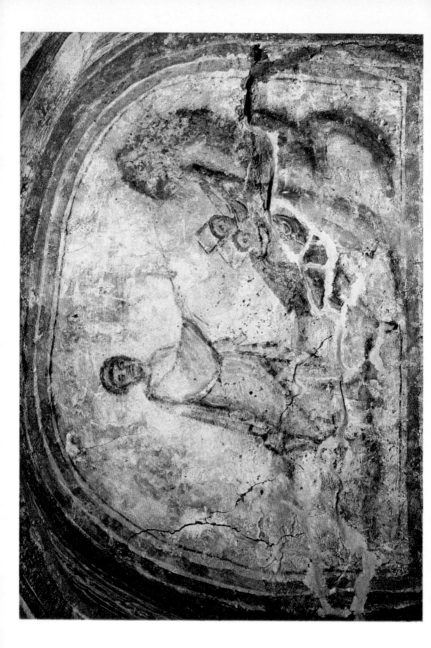

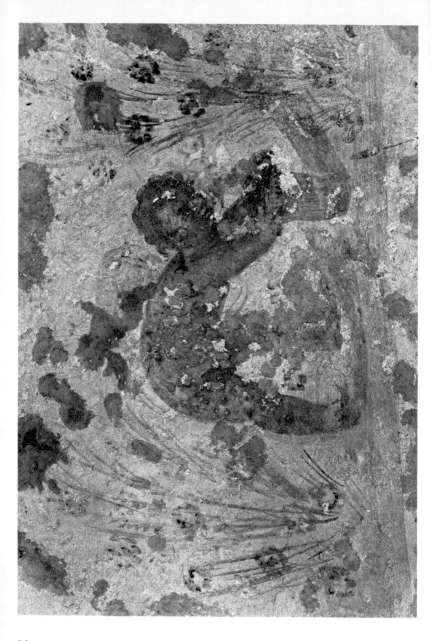

34

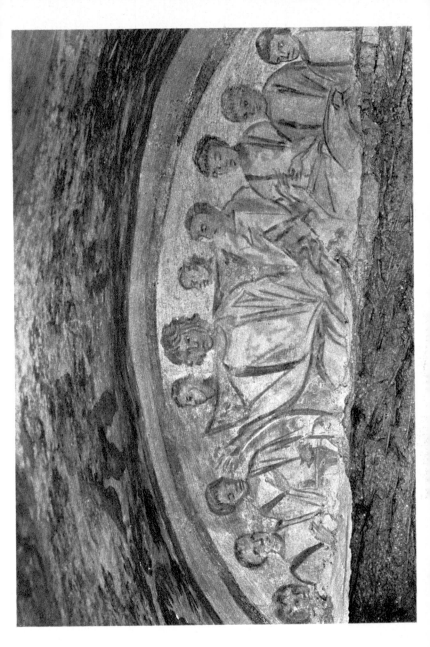

36

38

40

41

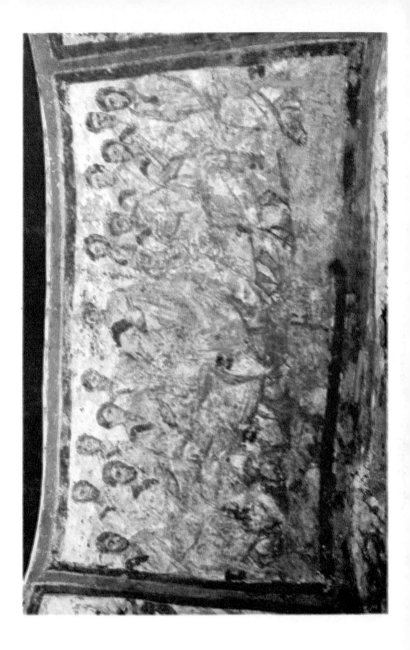

43

44

45

47

48

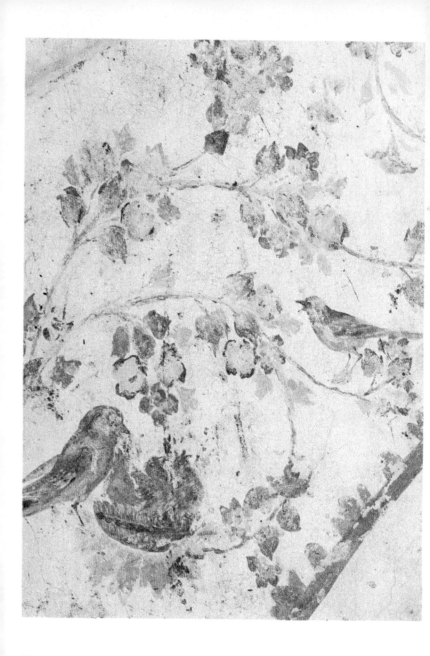

57

58

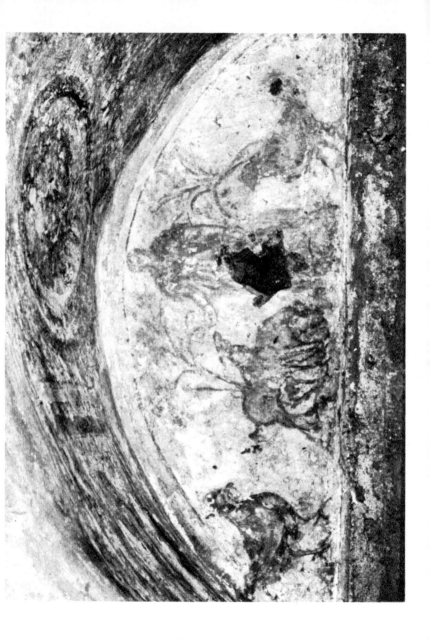

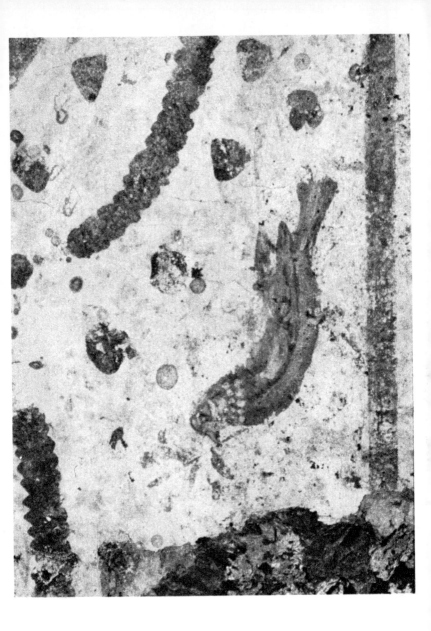

63

64

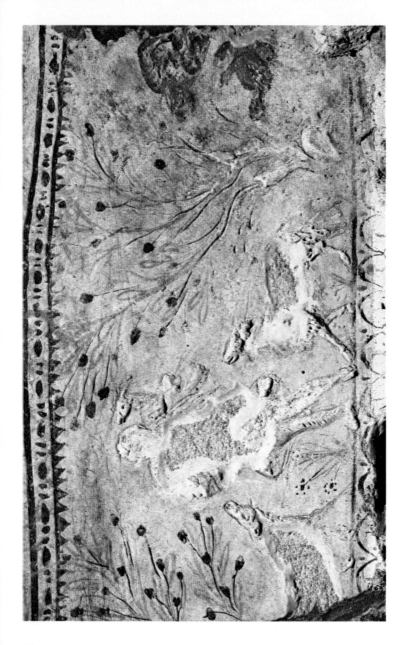

68

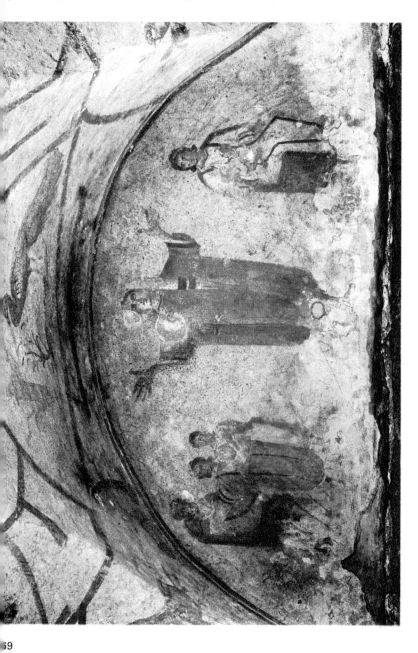

70

72

74

76

80

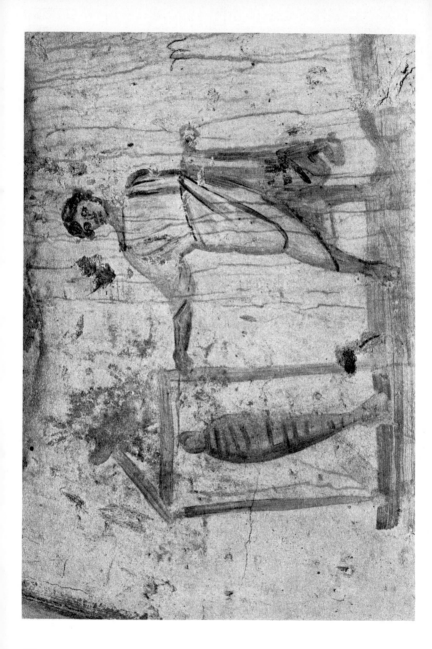

84

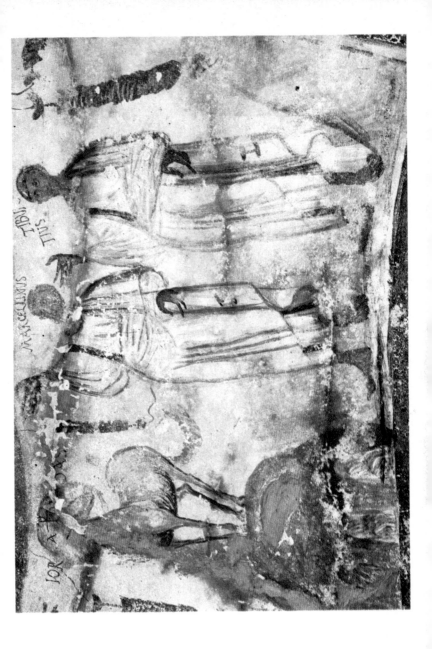

93

100

101

102

103

104

106

107

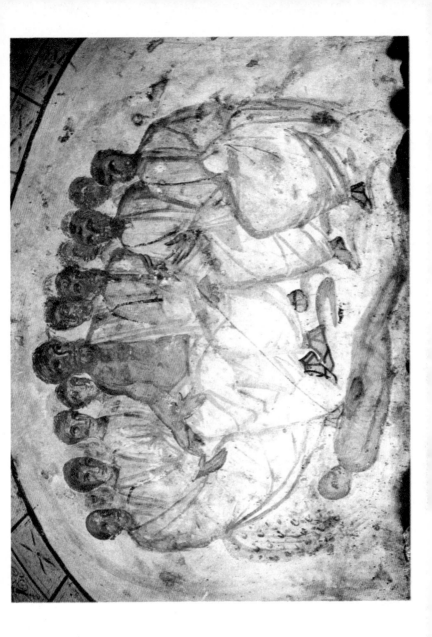

111

112

119

120

121

125

128

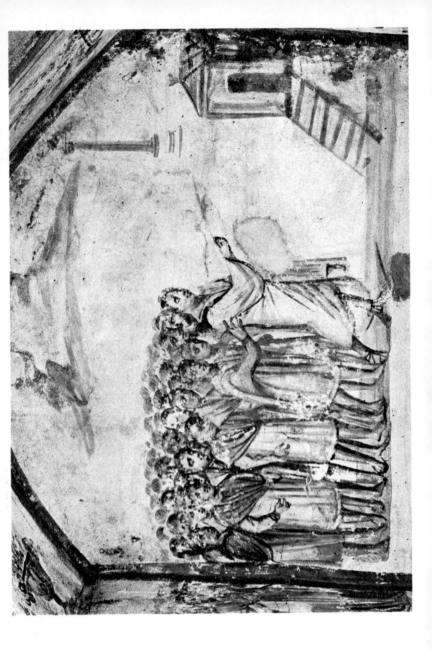

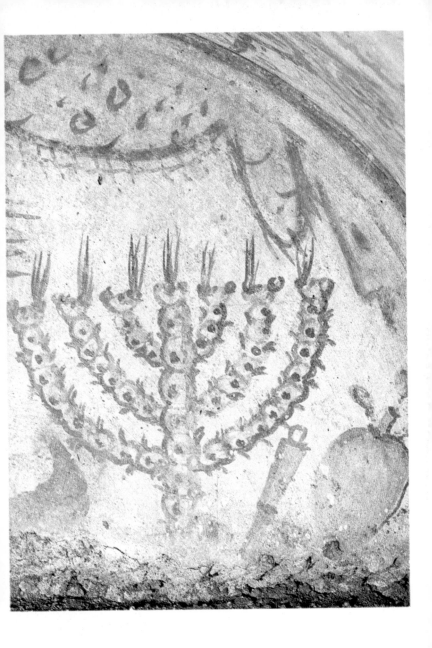

131

132

133

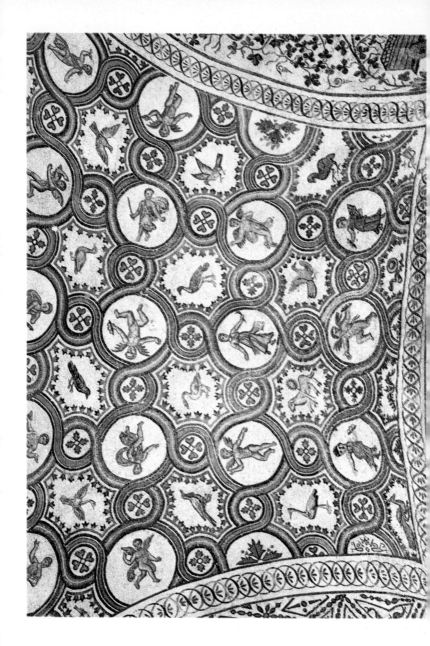

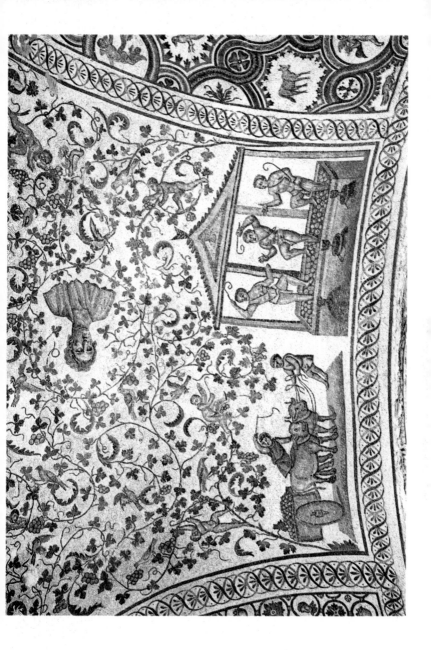

137

141

143

144

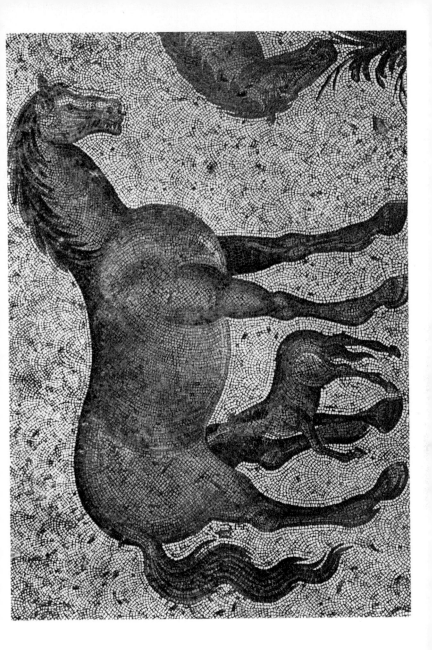

146

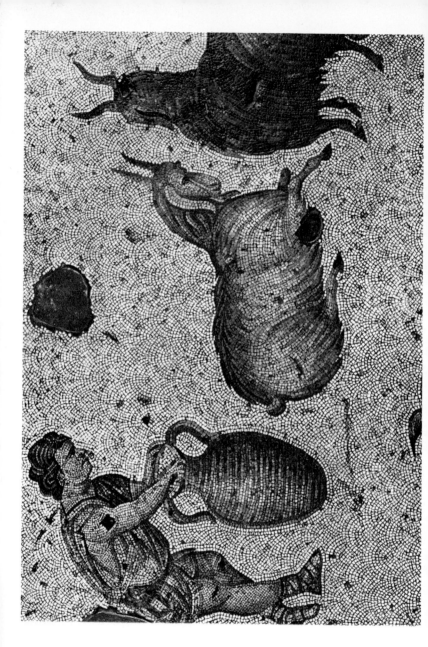

148

150

153

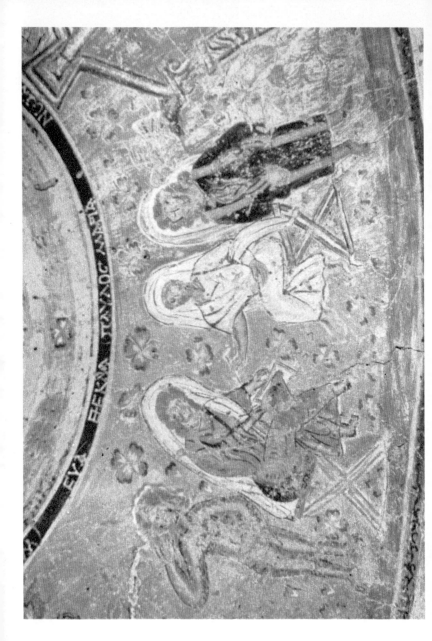

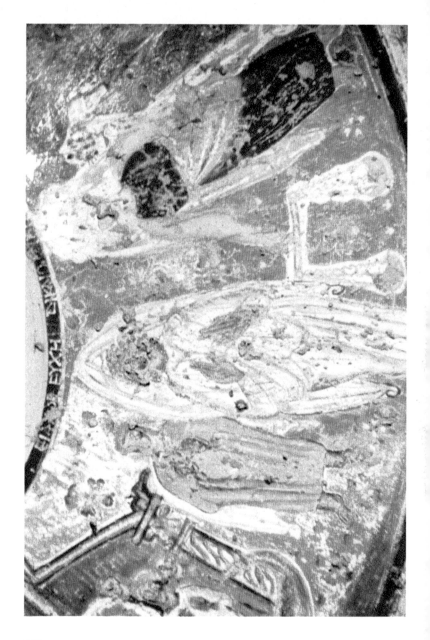

155

156

159

163

164

165

167

169

171

PRINCIPIODELUCXADIUNTPACEMOETERASARAS
EXQUIBUNTMACTANTLECTAS DEMOREBIDENTES
IUCIFERAECERERIISHOEBOOPATRIQUELYAEO
IUNONIANTEOMNISCUIUINCTAIUGALIACURAE
LESATINENSDEXTRASATATERAMTULCHIARIMADIDO
CANDENTESVACCAEALEDIAINTERCOAENUAFUNDIT

ALLTIISEXTQUIISAINIASRITESOLUTIS
AGGERECOMPOSITOTUMULTPOSTQUAMALTAQUIERINT
AEQUORATENDITITERUELISPORTUMQUERELINQUIT
KASTRANTAURATINNOCTEMNICCANDIDACURSUS
GRAMICASSPLENDENTIBIMULOSUBIUMINEPONTIS

175